I was blessed by *Some Days You Dance* a
found it to be not only very informative, but al
lady that cuts to the chase in life and will shov
you without having to be perfect all the time. Th
and will reveal things that people need to know so that they too can find their
way to freedom, just as Vikki did. I appreciate her candor and insight, and
highly recommend this book to you.

Jesse Duplantis
Author, Evangelist, Founder of Covenant Church

I love Vikki's new book, *Some Days You Dance*. She is so honest; she
has humbled herself and has bared her soul in order to help others enjoy the
same victorious lifestyle that she now enjoys. Vikki not only reveals her own
personal challenges and hardships—where God brought her from to where
she is today—she also shares the Bible-based principles that enabled her
(and will enable you) to overcome rejection, bitterness and self-deception.
She instructs you in how to lay aside the frantic "good works" that so many
Christians today are involved in, endeavoring to become accepted by the
Father, and instead shows you how to focus on just being who and what
His Word says you are—the righteousness of God, the sons and daughters
of God, and the heirs of God. I'm confident that as you read each page and
apply the truths that are revealed, your life will never be the same.

Dr. Jerry Savelle
Author, Minister, Founder of Heritage of Faith Christian Center

My friends Dennis and Vikki Burke model a standard of excellence for
the Body of Christ. *Some Days You Dance* is Vikki's remarkable testimony
of the power of God to transform a life. Whether you are weighed down by
the past or exhausted by your attempts to serve God, this book contains truth
that will point you to freedom, peace, and abundant life.

John Bevere,
Best-selling Author, Speaker
Messenger International

It's a "Genesis" moment when you face the hard truth....*Do I love this
life I live*? As you journey with Vikki through years of finding her answers to
freedom you will see and learn that...*YOU TOO can dance!*

Phil and Lynne Driscoll
Singer, Composer, Minister
Mighty Horn Ministries

My friend Vikki Burke is the one person I always thought had it all together! So reading her new book, *Some Days You Dance*, was shocking at first...and parts of it were so déjà vu , as if she was revealing parts of my own story as well, that's never been told. For years I was so busy performing and striving for perfection, but now I'm on "God's Love Assignment." Thank you Vikki for being so vulnerable by sharing your painful past and empowering the readers with God's Word. This book will challenge, inspire and heal anyone whose heart is open to God.

Anita Bryant
Entertainer, Author, former Miss Oklahoma
USO's Silver Medallion Award, Al Jolson Gold Medal Award,
Bob Hope Holiday Troupe

I have known Vikki Burke for more than twenty-five years, and her book is absolutely wonderful. Her honesty and transparency in sharing her testimony and the challenges of her journey of faith are a breath of fresh air. Every believer ought to read this book because it will help him or her avoid the trap of doing for God instead of first being with God. Vikki, you're a joy to know and an inspiration to me. Thank you for bearing your soul and sharing your journey with us. I love you.

Pat Harrison
President and Founder
Faith Christian Fellowship International Church Inc.

Surely this can't be so, I thought as I read Vikki Burke's openly exposing account of her life. As a teenager Vikki's spirit was rescued and set free by a new birth. Yet her pathetic past affected her soul (her mind, will, and emotions). Driven to overachieve, Vikki eventually burned out and crashed. But, led by her Savior, she followed Him to the place of peace for her soul. And in this extremely well written, reads-like-a-novel book, she reveals how deliverance came and how others can know complete victory and freedom.

Billye Brim
Billye Brim Ministries
Prayer Mountain of the Ozarks

I believe the message in this book will encourage you to live a life full of purpose and teach you how to enjoy the journey. I appreciate Vikki being so transparent in sharing her testimony of overcoming her past and learning how to enjoy life. I believe this is a right-on-time message and will teach you the steps to take to enjoy the freedom and victory that Jesus has purchased for you.

Mark Hankins
Mark Hankins Ministries

Vikki Burke has presented a rare and candid gift to the Body of Christ in *Some Days You Dance*. Her book spans denominational and non-denominational churches alike as easily as one might walk between two friends, who may be wearing different attire but ultimately going in the same direction. She writes of being honest with God and yourself, with stories that leap from the pages. She encourages every believer to get real with God and themselves, to see through the eyes of unconditional love and in so doing, break free into a new life of joy, power, peace and significance...just as the Lord had planned from the beginning of time.

Dr. Stephen and Kellie Swisher
Kenneth Copeland Ministries

I read Vikki's book with amazement. Her openness, transparency, willingness to "bare it all," plus provide the healing side of her story, will cause this book to be a source of strength and profound help to many readers who have "hit the wall" emotionally or who are physically exhausted and drained. I waited a long time for this book—and now that I've read it, I must say that it proved to reach higher than my expectations.

Rick Renner
Author, Pastor Good News Church
Moscow, Russia

Vikki fleshes out for us all what it is to find the kind of freedom our faith promises, but many fail to achieve. Her spiritual journey is shared with great courage and candor, wisdom and wit. I see it as a roadmap for anyone willing to begin their own journey toward true freedom in Christ. I loved it!

Ava Pickard, MSSW, LCSW
Christian Therapist, Healing Streams Ministries

I was captivated from the opening paragraph! What surprised me was to see "my story" between the lines. After a few years of dancing through my own tears...I found that I was the one screaming, "I'm so glad that I'm saved and going to heaven and all, BUT IT APPEARS THERE IS STILL SOMETHING VERY WRONG WITH ME!" Whether a new believer or seasoned minister, you will find yourself between the lines of each page. It's a MUST READ for every believer (and I believe this book would lead any nonbeliever to our loving God)! Don't skip the Discovery Guide! Powerful and liberating!

Neecie Moore, Ph.D.
LMFT - Licensed Marriage & Family Therapist
LPCS - Licensed Professional Counselor Supervisor
Clinical Member AAMFT (American Association of
Marriage & Family Therapists)

I don't read many books other than the Bible. About the only topics I'm interested in are business and politics—NOT human interest or biographical books. My wife was so impressed and positively affected by *Some Days You Dance* that I could not help but pick it up just to scan through it, but instead I read every page! It is a powerful book that has the capacity to touch the heart and minister to the needs of every man or woman who reads it. Vikki's willingness to provide such an open and honest revelation of her own life should be an encouragement to all of us to deal with our own *self-imposed* shortcomings and thereby position ourselves to truly live in the freedom and complete prosperity God desires for us. No one should miss this book. It will BLESS you—even if you are a political junkie or businessman who normally would never read a book like this—in fact, especially if that's the case!

Buddy Pilgrim
Former President of Pilgrim's Pride Corp.
Minister, Entrepreneur

Some Days You Dance will bless and encourage you to keep pressing into Jesus the author and finisher of your faith, so that you walk in a greater understanding of who you are in Christ and to train and reign in the area of your mind.

Rev. Margaret Court AO, MBE, Ph.D. LLD (hon)
Senior Pastor, Victory Life Centre
International Tennis Hall of Fame
Perth, Western Australia

Vikki Burke has written a true masterpiece! This book addresses the heart of the battle for so many people, including those of us in ministry. I hope every Christian everywhere will read this book and allow it to minister to their heart. Vikki has over thirty years experience understanding this battle—AND she has found the victory! May you find your freedom as well. This may very well be the spiritual medicine you need to put you over. Job well done, Vikki.

Mark T. Barclay
Author, Pastor, Living Word Church

Some Days You Dance is a revealing story of the power and love of God as it transforms the life and family of Vikki Burke. I both wept and cheered as Vikki overcomes her desperation and eventually triumphs over evil. This is a must read book for anyone who wants to experience the life changing power of God.

Pastor Happy Caldwell
Agape Church
Little Rock, Arkansas

Most people, including myself, can relate to trying to earn worth and value through accomplishments and tireless efforts to please everyone—including God. Having experienced rejection and abuse myself, Vikki's words are an echo of my past, and it was exciting to read about her journey to freedom. Her story is gripping and will have you anticipating the words on the next page as to how she details her journey to freedom. She outlines the practical steps for anyone who wants to put the past behind them, once and for all. This book is a "must read" for every person who desires to be free—free from performing at life, free from insecurity, free from debilitating thoughts, free from struggle. It's also a great tool to use to minister to others.

Terri Savelle Foy
CEO Jerry Savelle Ministries

When is enough enough? Approval addiction, performance based behavior and a search for acceptance is a prescription for a life of self defeat. In *Some Days You Dance* insightful author Vikki Burke draws a blueprint for a purposed-filled path to freedom and victory. Her book is life changing and a much needed breath of fresh air. I highly recommend it.

Van Crouch
Best-selling Author, Motivational Speaker for Fortune 500 Companies
President, Van Crouch Communications

Some Days You Dance

FINDING THE WAY TO FREEDOM

by Vikki Burke

Foreword by Kenneth Copeland

What an outstanding book! Seeing people set totally free by the power and love of Jesus became the very core of my life after having been in this ministry for 45 years and witnessing first-hand the ministry of healing and deliverance of my spiritual father, Oral Roberts. *Some Days You Dance* stirred me to that core. The devil tries his best to tear down every believer's life one way or another. If he can't keep you from answering the call of God in your life, he'll try to use you up by luring you into your own plans and ways instead of THE plan and THE way that God has for you. Well, Vikki has jerked the wraps off the tricks and lies that he used to try and destroy her and everything dear to her heart.

Gloria and I have known Vikki and Dennis Burke well over 35 years. I could have saved the devil a lot of trouble and defeat by telling him to let Vikki Burke and her family alone. She not only by faith defeated him, she has written this fine book revealing to you and me how the Lord Jesus taught her and gave her this great victory. He is no respecter of persons. His Word works for anyone who will put it to work. Vikki did that. The Word worked. She is a free woman! The apostle John wrote it like this, "And this is the victory that overcomes the world, even our faith." When you read *Some Days You Dance*, read every page knowing this same world-overcoming faith that set Vikki Burke free, is just as much yours as it is hers. It's all in Jesus and comes by hearing, and hearing the Word of God. It's FAITH IN GOD.

Unless otherwise indicated, all Scripture quotations are taken from the *New Living Translation* of the Bible, copyright © 1996, 2004, 2007 by Tyndale House Foundation, Carol Stream, Illinois 60188.

New American Standard Bible © The Lockman Foundation 1960, 1962, 1963, 1968, 1972, 1973, 1975, 1977, La Habra, California.

The Amplified Bible © The Lockman Foundation, La Habra, California, 1954, 1958.

The New Testament in Modern English (Phillips). Rev. Ed. © 1958, 1959, 1960, 1972 by J.B. Phillips. Published by Macmillan Publishing Co., New York, New York.

The Living Bible © 1971 by Tyndale House Publishers, Inc., Wheaton, Illinois.

New International Version © 1973, 1978, 1984 by International Bible Society.

The Heart of Paul © 1976 by Ben Campbell Johnson. Published by A Great Love, Inc., Toccoa, Georgia.

Some Days You Dance
ISBN 978-1-936314-73-7
© 2011 by Vikki Burke
PO Box 150043
Arlington, TX 76015

Published by Word & Spirit Publishing
P.O. Box 701403
Tulsa, OK   74170
wordandspiritpublishing.com

Text Design: Lisa Simpson

All rights reserved. None of this book may be reproduced or transmitted in any form or by any means, electronic or mechanical, including photocopying, recording or by any information storage and retrieval system, without the written permission of the publisher. Printed in Canada.

TABLE OF CONTENTS

CHAPTER 1

Singing to the Wall

The young women will dance for joy, and the men— old and young—will join in the celebration. I will turn their mourning into joy. I will comfort them and exchange their sorrow for rejoicing.

Jeremiah 31:13 NLT

Most of us don't know when the dancing stopped. For some of us, like me, it happened so early that we can't remember we ever danced at all.

But we did. Every single one of us.

It's taken years and a journey I never dreamed possible to be sure this is true. But I can say now, without any doubt, that God himself put a sparkle in the eye and a dance in the heart of every child ever born. He created us all to be so free, so loved, so full of joy that life itself is a celebration.

One of my favorite preachers who hears the Lord as accurately as anybody I've ever known says that God once told him this: *If it hadn't been for sin, I would never have had a serious thought. I would have spent eternity just having fun with My children.* What a great thought! Fun and fellowship with God and each other forever. Such was God's desire for us from the beginning, and such would be the story of our lives if things had gone along unspoiled.

But the fact is, they didn't. Somewhere along the way, for all of us, the storyline got changed. Our freedom was stolen. The fun began to fade. The pickpocketing devil slipped in and pilfered it so subtly and slowly that we hardly even noticed what was happening. For the most part (especially in our early years), he used ordinary people and the every-day events to get the job done. A schoolmate's harsh remark. A parent, weary from the workday, lashing out at us for a foolish mistake. A teacher, stretched to the limit, criticizing us for being too boisterous, too slow, or too shy.

Normal experiences of childhood, right? We all have them. They're no big deal. We take them so much for granted as they pile up year after year that we don't realize how they're changing us. How with each rejection or humiliation, we withdraw a little more to protect ourselves. How with each failure or criticism, we become a little less adventurous, a little less alive, a little less free to be ourselves.

For some people the process is gentle and gradual. For others it's rough and rapid. There's truth to the saying, *Hurting people hurt people.* So when you grow up as I did, sur-rounded by the seriously wounded, your liberty is stripped in more dramatic ways. Instead of slipping in as a pickpocket, the devil barrels in and robs you at gunpoint. (In my particu-lar case, that's more literal than figurative.)

But, either way, nobody escapes completely unscathed. Even in the most healthy, loving families, "the thief comes… to steal, and kill, and destroy," (John 10:10 NASB), and if you know what to look for, the evidence is there.

A friend of mine spotted it recently in her own family. It surfaced during the annual gathering of her relatives from around the country to celebrate the holidays. In honor of the occasion, my friend asked her oldest granddaughter, a chirpy 11-year-old who's always loved to sing, to entertain the group with a tune or two.

The year before, the girl had jumped at the chance. She'd serenaded the same familial bunch with uninhibited glee. But this time it was different. A tinge of scarlet spread across her fair, freckled face. She hung her head as if guilty of some minor crime and said, "No."

"But we all want to hear you!" her mother pleaded.

Eyes fixed on the carpet, the girl shook her blonde head. Every adult in the room understood what she was feeling. She was afraid of making a mistake and looking the fool. She'd grown up some since last year, watched enough music videos and episodes of *American Idol* to be embarrassed about her vocal imperfections. The family thought she was wonderful and talented, but she was no longer sure of it herself. So she decided to play it safe. She hid her inadequacies by refusing to sing.

Uncles, aunts, and cousins accepted her decision with good humor and went back to football and pumpkin pie. Her grandmother, however, was less easily dissuaded. (You know how grandmothers are.) After extensive wheedling, she convinced her granddaughter to grant her a private performance in another room. But even there, standing in front of the one person in the world in whose eyes she could do no wrong, the little songstress couldn't relax. So she turned her back toward her grandmother, faced the other way, and sang in a timid voice...looking at the wall.

As she was singing, another admirer joined the audience—my friend's younger granddaughter, a wide-eyed three-year-old. She listened to her older cousin, breathless with admiration, and when the song was over, clapped her dimpled hands. "My turn!" she cried.

Rushing to stand beside her cousin, the toddler tried to follow her example by turning away from her grandmother and singing to the wall. But she couldn't do it. Her joy overcame her. The more she sang, belting out words and a tune that she made up as she went along, the more exuberant she became. Waving her arms, she whirled and giggled and called out between choruses, "Watch my moves, Grandma! Watch my moves!"

A few of the adults in the other room heard the ruckus and, filtering in to enjoy the show, marveled at it. None of them could remember what it felt like to be that free. To feel so unconditionally loved. So perfectly accepted. So delighted with themselves and everybody else.

Like the rest of us, they all lost that kind of freedom long ago. So long ago, that they don't even really notice it's gone.

What if?

But what if it was possible for us to regain that kind of freedom?

What if we could grow back into our lost liberty the same way we grew out of it, not all at once in the kind of magic wand moment you find in fairy tales but a little at a time... day by day, month by month, and year by year? What if Someone came along who could undo the damage that's been done to our heart, restore what the devil has stolen, and set us free? Totally free.

Like we were in the beginning.

I know it sounds unrealistic but, if we believe the Bible, we must be willing to at least entertain the possibility. After all, it does say that "For this purpose the Son of God was manifested, that He might destroy the works of the devil" (1 John 3:8). It does tell us that Jesus came to restore our lost freedom. He said it Himself, again and again:

- ...you shall know the truth, and the truth shall make you free (John 8:32).

- ...if the Son makes you free, you shall be free indeed (v. 36).

- I have come that they may have life, and that they may have it more abundantly (John 10:10).

- The Spirit of the LORD is upon Me, Because He has anointed Me to...heal the brokenhearted, to proclaim liberty to the captives...to set at liberty those who are oppressed (Luke 4:18).

None of us who consider ourselves Christians would ever argue with those verses. In fact, most of us believe we already have what they promise. We would say we're free. But we'd mean it in more of a theological sense. We'd mean that we've been freed from the spiritual penalty of sin; that we're free to go to heaven instead of hell when we die; that we're no longer held captive by some of the grosser sins that enslaved us before we were saved.

But are we as liberated as a dancing, singing three-year-old? Are we so void of any sense of shame, inferiority, unworthiness, or fear that we can whirl through life enjoying God, ourselves, and everybody around us? Are we so free to be who we are, so confident of the divine love and acceptance flowing to us from above that we can say, "Watch my moves, Heavenly Father! Watch my moves!"

Uh…well…not so much.

Most of us, even after we're saved, continue to shuffle through life shackled (at least partially) by the same emotional chains that have bound us since childhood. We try our best to ignore them. We try to live out our faith with boldness and confidence, but it's hard to do because we're still so afraid of making mistakes and revealing our shortcomings. Even though we're born again on the inside, on the outside we're still coping with our insecurities, much still like my friend's 11-year-old granddaughter did—by singing to the wall.

We don't talk about it much in church, though. I'm not sure why. Maybe it's because wall singers blend so beautifully into organized religion that nobody notices there's a problem.

After all, wall singers don't make waves. They keep a low profile. They go with the flow. They work tirelessly on committees, in church nurseries, and at bake sales. They wear themselves out to please God and other people, hoping to prove somehow that they really are valuable and acceptable despite their embarrassing imperfections.

Wall singers also try to make everybody around them comfortable. They keep silent about their inner struggles, greeting fellow believers each Sunday with sanctified smiles and sideways hugs. They don't make a fuss about how weary and inadequate they feel, how disappointed and unfulfilled. After all, nobody else seems to feel that way. Everybody else looks like they have it all together.

Of course, you know as well as I do, that's because we all don our emotional best before stepping into the sanctuary on Sunday morning. No believer in his right mind wears the rags of his personal pain to something as polished as a church service. Nobody is going to flaunt their flaws in front of people whose greatest shortcoming appears to be that they say *Praise the Lord!* too often and with too much zeal.

Just imagine what an uproar would ensue if, even once, some believer—not a lost sinner but a born-again saint— waxed bold enough to blurt out in front of everybody, "I'm glad that I'm saved and going to heaven and all, BUT IT APPEARS THERE IS STILL SOMETHING VERY WRONG WITH ME!"

I'm not suggesting anybody should do that, you understand. But it's interesting to think what might happen. The stunned silence that would follow. The looks of relief on the faces of congregation members (who've struggled with the same feelings) as they mutter, "I know what you mean, brother. Me too!" The worship leader, in an earnest endeavor to encourage everyone, plunging into an impromptu rendition of the old Andre Crouch song, "Jesus is the answer for the world today..."

In all seriousness, that would be the perfect song for the occasion. It's awesome and it's true. Jesus *is* the answer. He's the answer to every significant question in our lives. He's the solution to every painful problem. He's the complete cure, not only for the sin that darkens our spirit but for the pain that has crippled our soul.

The problem is, most of us don't go to Him about that pain. Having secured through Him our eternity in heaven, we don't bother Him too much with our emotional messes here on earth. We're not sure it would do any good even if we did. When we look around and see how good everybody else seems to be doing, we can't help but wonder if we're slightly more defective than they are.

Maybe there's something extra wrong with me, we think. *Maybe I'm so broken that not even Jesus can fix me. It's a good thing He accepts me "just as I am," because it looks like just as I am is how I will always be.*

Asking the Hard Questions

"I don't know what you're talking about, Vikki," somebody might say, "I've never had those kinds of thoughts."

Maybe that's good. Maybe you've already found the path to freedom.

Or then again, maybe you're like I used to be. For the first few decades of my Christian life, I was absolutely oblivious to my own broken condition. Back then, I was in total denial. I was so busy doing the millions of things a good Christian and minister must do to be "a good Christian and minister," that I had no time for introspection. I didn't even notice anything was wrong with me. I just assumed that anybody who could work as hard and get so much done "for the Lord" as I did must be doing just fine, thank you very much.

Free?

Of course, I was free.

At least that's what I thought. Until one day, I sank into a sea of spiritual exhaustion. It was only then as I found myself slipping beneath waves of depression, weighed down by the chains of shame, blame, fear, and guilt the devil had fastened on me years before, that I realized I wasn't just fine. It was only when I was too tired to swim another spiritual stroke, and so angry at God that I shook my fist in His face practically daring Him to rescue me, that I started asking the hard questions. Questions like:

- What's wrong with my life?

- Why are my relationships so disappointing?

- Why do I always try to please people instead of just being myself?

- Why am I so frustrated, angry, and insecure?

- Why am I so afraid of failure and rejection?

- Why don't I enjoy the kind of peace, joy and fulfillment the Bible promises?

- Why is life so hard?

At the time, I was ashamed to have such questions. But not anymore. Now I know that every believer who wants to enjoy the true freedom Jesus offers must ask them. All of us must first face the truth about our own captivity before we can get a revelation of the Truth that sets us free. We must admit we have a problem before Jesus can give us the answer.

Personally, I came to the point where I had to acknowledge my problems or die. So I got honest—gut-wrenchingly, soul-searchingly honest about the painful past I'd tried to forget, and the performance-driven present that I'd pretended was normal.

It's one thing to be that honest with yourself and with God. It's another to be that way with everybody else. Especially in print. So, 20 years after I took that first step on my journey to freedom, when I decided to write this book and share what I've discovered, I set that kind of honesty aside. In the initial who-knows-how-many drafts, I stuck with the role of the teacher, explaining the Scriptural truths that changed my life like I do in Bible school, line by line and precept by precept. Sure, I sprinkled in a few personal anecdotes to illustrate my points, but mostly I shared the good parts of my story—the parts that took no courage to tell.

After writing (and rewriting…and rewriting) the first few chapters, however, I sensed something wasn't right. I called an editor friend of mine for help and she ruined my plan. She dared me to do more than simply teach what I've learned. She suggested that anybody who wants to experience the freedom I've found will have to start by looking as honestly at their lives as I have.

"That can be scary for some of us," she said. "We're afraid to look at the pain in our past. Afraid we'll get stuck in it. Afraid that even Jesus won't be able to take it away and make us whole again."

She had a point. Getting that real is like jumping off the high dive when you're a kid. It's easier if somebody else goes first. Once you see how they did it, once you see them whooping and hollering in the swimming pool about how fun it was, you want to jump in too.

Still, I had reservations about that kind of self disclosure. While I pondered them, my friend plunged on. "Vikki, will you be transparent about what you've been through?" she asked. "Ministers are often reluctant to do that. They're comfortable sharing their successes but not their struggles. They're hesitant to acknowledge just how human they can be. Will you go there? Will you be absolutely real—both emotionally and spiritually—so that others can make the jump that you did to get free?"

Cutting the Strings

As you are about to see, my answer turned out to be yes.

22

In the pages that follow, I share in a far more personal way than I originally intended what the Lord has taught me about regaining our lost freedom. I not only share the revelations that have revolutionized my life, I take you with me on my journey. I tell my story with more candor than is comfortable to help get you thinking and talking to God about the uncomfortable parts of your own story. I reveal myself—imperfections and all—because I believe that, as Christians, we should be free enough to let down our hair and be real with God, with ourselves, and with each other.

And somebody has to go first.

I'll admit, the idea is unconventional. Normally, only celebrities tell their stories. And I am definitely no celebrity. I'm not a Paris Hilton whose adventures fascinate because she's, well, *Paris Hilton.* My husband and I have a fruitful international ministry and I'm grateful for it, but the vast majority of humankind has never heard of us. (Trust me, we can safely go to Walmart without people staring at us and whispering, "Isn't that Vikki and Dennis Burke?" No problem there.)

I'm not telling my story because it's so astoundingly spectacular, either. I haven't died, gone to heaven, and come back to tell about it. I haven't landed a disabled airplane on the Hudson River. I haven't given birth to octuplets. My story is more like yours. It's marked by the kinds of challenges we all face, the kinds of pain we all feel, and the kind of victory we can all have if we'll get real enough with Jesus.

Stories like that may not make headlines on the evening news, but they're important nonetheless. They matter. Especially to God. According to Psalm 56:8, He tracks every step of our life's journey, saves the tears we cry, and records our sorrows in a book. His thoughts about us are too numerous to count, more than the sands of the sea (Psalm 40:5; 139:187).

It's no wonder the Bible contains so many stories! God thinks they're important. He included hundreds of them in the Scriptures because He knows how much we can learn from them.

I'm not suggesting, of course, that your story and mine should be added to the sacred Canon. But I am saying they're divinely significant. Almighty God, the Creator of the Universe, cares a great deal about them. He knows every detail of what's happened in our lives. He remembers, with greater clarity than we do, the events of our journey thus far. He understands how those events have affected us and He wants to talk to us about it. He wants to help us see those events in a whole new light.

God's light shining on our past makes all the difference in our future.

Many Christians never find that out. Accepting a superficial interpretation of 2 Corinthians 5:17, "...old things have passed away; behold, all things have become new," they slam the door on their past. They assume they're free of it just because they've become Christians. Yet, all the while, things that happened to them long ago in the tender years of childhood are pulling their strings. Mindsets and patterns, set in place when the devil first started stealing their freedom, manipulate them like puppet masters from some dimly lit place in their soul.

I know what that's like.

So do you.

Because we all start our Christian life in that condition. As captives to our past, as marionettes on strings.

But, thank God, we don't have to stay that way. We can learn to take the sword of the Spirit which is the Word of God and sever those strings. We can fellowship with Jesus, find out the Truth, and apply it on purpose to the specific areas where we've been bound. We can, with the help of the Holy Spirit, cut ourselves free.

In a nutshell, this book is about how to do that. It's about how the cutting-free process works—not just how it worked in my life but how it can work in yours. Nestled in these chapters are truths that can lift you into a whole new relationship with God. Whether you're discovering those truths for the first time, or rediscovering them more fully, they can liberate you in a way you never dreamed possible. They can help you see in a clearer light who you really are, how deeply you are loved, and how free God created you to be.

Getting Rid of the Weeds

I do want to warn you, however, that truth isn't all you should be looking for as you read these pages. If you really want to find your road to freedom, there's something else you need to identify as well. You must begin to uncover, just as I did, the hidden deceptions, confusion, and fears the devil has used to keep you bound.

Many believers don't realize it, but identifying the lies we've believed and getting rid of them is just as vital as hearing the truth. Jesus made that clear in Mark 4, where He told the parable of the sower. There, He compared hearing the Word to planting seed in the ground and said:

"The sower sows the word. And these are the ones who are beside the road where the word is sown; and when they hear, immediately Satan comes and takes away the word which has been sown in them. And in a

similar way these are the ones on whom seed was sown on the rocky places, who, when they hear the word, immediately receive it with joy; and they have no firm root in themselves, but are only temporary; then, when affliction or persecution arises because of the word, immediately they fall away. And others are the ones on whom seed was sown among the thorns; these are the ones who have heard the word, and the worries of the world, and the deceitfulness of riches, and the desires for other things enter in and choke the word, and it becomes unfruitful (verses 16-20).

The four kinds of soil Jesus talks about in those verses represent four kinds of hearts. And, whether we like to admit it or not, we can all identify with each one. At one time or another, most of us as believers have experienced each of the heart conditions Jesus listed.

Notice that the first two kinds of soil were hard, like the dirt on an unpaved road or a rocky path. That kind of ground has been packed down by pressure. It's been walked on and run over again and again.

Have you ever felt like you've been walked on? Have you ever felt like your heart has been run over so many times that you'll never recover? If so, it's important to get honest about that and ask God to help you, because Jesus said when we're in that condition, the seed of God's Word will bounce right off of us. His truth won't penetrate our hearts at all.

This is sad, but it's a fact: there are multitudes of believers sitting in church every Sunday who've been hurt so badly that they've stopped trusting anybody. They won't open their hearts because they're trying to protect themselves from further pain. As a result, the Word of God goes in one ear and out the other. Even if they remember it, even if they can recite everything the pastor said and every verse he quoted, that Word won't affect their lives. It won't bear the fruit of joy, peace, and freedom it's designed to produce.

The third kind of soil Jesus described has weeds in it. It's overrun with wicked thorns that choke out the Word before it can grow. Where do such weeds come from? I guarantee you that they don't just spring up on their own. They're put there in seed form by the devil himself.

He plants them inside us in our early years, when he sets about to steal our freedom. Instead of just taking our treasure; he leaves something in exchange. He pilfers our faith and peace, and replaces them with fear and turmoil. He robs us of our confidence in God's love and our sense of worth and leaves us with feelings of rejection and inadequacy. He takes the truth and exchanges it for a lie. When those lies grow up, they become the thorns Jesus described as *the worries or cares of this world, the deceitfulness of riches, and lusts for other things.*

Think about it and you can easily see how the process works. The lie, planted during the disappointments of youth, that we can't trust God to take care of us, eventually grows into a weed of financial anxiety and leaves Philippians 4:19[1] sounding like a fairy tale. The lie that we're unacceptable, born from early feelings of rejection, deafens us to 1 John 3:1[2] and drives us like slaves to please other people and prove our value. The lie that we need something else to make us whole and happy so blinds us to the truth of Colossians 2:10,[3] that we bust our budget wide open buying things to make us feel better about ourselves.

---

[1] "And my God shall supply all your need according to His riches in glory by Christ Jesus."
[2] "Behold what manner of love the Father has bestowed on us, that we should be called children of God!"
[3] "and you are complete in Him, who is the head of all principality and power."

What can we do about weeds like that?

First, let me tell you what we *shouldn't* do about them. We shouldn't deal with them by simply lopping the tops off them. I don't know about you, but I've tried that. I've spotted thorny attitudes in my heart and tried to rid myself of them by addressing the outward symptoms and adhering to a list of *don'ts*. Don't worry about money. Don't spend so much time at the office. Don't make so many trips to the mall.

Maybe you've tried that too. If you have, you know what happens. It's like chopping the top off the weeds in your lawn. It does no good. They grow right back. To banish weeds completely, you have to deal with the roots. It's the only way to get free of them once and for all.

That's why I want to encourage you to dialogue with the Holy Spirit about the personal discoveries you begin to make as you read this book. Let Him talk to you about how to specifically and personally apply the Scriptural truths you encounter. Ask Him to reveal the hidden lies that could keep those truths from bearing fruit in your life and let Him help you deal with those lies—at the root.

If you're not sure how to do that, don't worry about it. I'll give you plenty of illustrations from my own life to get you started. In the following chapters, you'll have the chance to learn from (laugh at, cry over, and be inspired by) specific examples of how God has helped me deal with the soil of my own heart.

You'll see how He took the rototiller of Truth and softened my soul when it was as hard as a dirt road run over by a fleet of 18-wheelers. You'll find out how He uprooted mindsets that kept me in bondage for years. You'll see in my life the same weed seeds of shame, blame, guilt, and fear the devil plants in us all—seeds that eventually grew up and stunted my fellowship with God, imprisoned me in a works-driven form of Christianity, and kept me hiding in the shadows. Best of all, you'll see how I learned to attack those weeds with the Word and kill them graveyard dead.

I've chosen to share my story here because I believe that stories teach. Sometimes they teach better than sermons or classroom lectures or textbooks. But, because much of what I've learned came to me while studying to teach a Bible School course, you'll also find this is a *how-to book*. It includes instructions that will help you renew your mind with the Word, speak that Word in faith and power, and put it into practical action in your everyday life. To get the most out of it, you'll want to check out the study guide at the back. Answer the questions and let them stimulate your thinking. Use them as tools to help you get started in your dialogue with God.

You might also consider gathering up a few friends who are willing to take this journey with you. Go through the book together. Share your stories. Learn from each other. Pray with each other. Get real together and find out how liberating it can be.

Can I promise that by the time you finish this book you'll be as free as a singing, laughing three-year-old? No. But I can promise this: If you apply what you learn here and let the Lord help you, you'll start moving in that direction. You'll get on the road that leads to liberty. If you keep following it day after day, month after month, and year after year, you'll find yourself regaining the freedom we all lost long ago—the freedom that was stolen not just during the tender years of our childhood, but thousands of years earlier. In the Garden of Eden.

Jesus meant it when He said, "... if the Son makes you free, you shall be free indeed." He really can take you on a journey, back to the place where every Christian, in their deepest heart, longs to live. A place where you're so free and so full of joy in the light of His love that, some days, you dance.

I know because He did it for me.

CHAPTER 2

A Failed Journey of Inches

Now may the God of peace Himself sanctify you completely; and may your whole spirit, soul, and body be preserved blameless at the coming of our Lord Jesus Christ. He who calls you is faithful, who also will do it.
1 Thessalonians 5:23-24

Sometimes the gospel must journey thousands of miles to change a life. Other times, it must only travel few inches.

Most of us know how important the miles are, how vital the missionary treks that bring the message of redemption to remote jungles or forgotten villages. But do we realize, I wonder, just how crucial the inches can be? Do we understand that for the truth to set people free, it must not only travel around the world and across continents, it must make that all-important 18-inch journey from the head to the heart?

I'll be the first to admit, there was a time in my life when I didn't. There was a time when I was so busy getting the Word out to others that I didn't even notice it wasn't getting into me—penetrating down deep into the bedrock of my soul—the way it should.

When my well-ordered Christian life crumbled, I had a head full of Scriptural knowledge. I understood quite well (or thought I did) my identity as a child of God. I knew that Jesus died on the cross to save us all from sin. I believed that through Him I had been cleansed from guilt, made right with God, and crowned a joint-heir with Christ.

Although I wasn't keen on preaching back then, in a pinch I could deliver a message that was as Scriptural as they come. I could talk about how, as Christians, we've been made new creatures, how old things have passed away and all things have become new. I could tell you how to live by faith and give you Biblical keys to everything from receiving healing to raising your kids.

It was all good stuff. I loved it and knew without question that it was true.

From the time I first heard the gospel as a 19-year-old girl, I believed everything I found in the Bible. I embraced with childlike confidence Scriptural realities that staggered more skeptical minds. I also found out that such simple faith could cause me all kinds of trouble.

Not long after I was born again, for instance, it pretty much cost me my job. I worked at the University of Southern California in the Sociology Department at the time, transcribing for a group of professors who studied and wrote books on marriage. For the most part, I was a quiet employee and everybody there had always liked me just fine. But that changed the day I applied my newfound faith in an unusual way.

An intern had offered me the opportunity to take a survey routinely given to people who came in for counseling. I did it just for fun, never dreaming the stir I was about to create.

The next day, after I turned in the survey to be evaluated, everyone started avoiding me. They wouldn't even make eye contact. Baffled, I mustered the courage to ask one of the interns about it. Her response stunned me. "Why, you're the biggest liar we've ever seen," she said. "There were seven questions on the survey to which everybody, if they're honest, must answer *yes*. You marked every one of them *no*."

I knew right away what had happened. I'd answered the questions based on my short experience as a Christian. I believed so literally that I'd become a new person when I gave my life to Jesus that I saw my past as non-existent. So I filled out the survey as if I had none.

When asked if I'd ever stolen anything, even something as small as a pencil from my employer, I answered *no*. Asked if I'd ever lied, I said *no*. There was no way to explain my vanished past to my employers, of course. They would never understand. To them I would always be the liar who couldn't be trusted. My employment at USC ended shortly thereafter.

For years I chuckled when I remembered how naive I'd been to reveal my simple faith in such a silly way. Yet it never dawned on me that my real mistake had been much more serious. I had failed to distinguish between the re-creation of the spirit and the transforming of the soul.

You may have done the same thing when you were first saved. Many baby Christians do. Most of us, in the first few years of our Christian life, aren't taught to differentiate soul and spirit. As a result, we misinterpret 2 Corinthians 5:17: "…if anyone is in Christ, he is a new creation; old things have passed away; behold, all things have become new." We take the verse to mean, *From this day forward, everything will be perfect. You won't have any problems. You'll always be happy. Your past is gone. It will never affect you again.*

We're right, of course, to believe the verse means what it says—that the regeneration of our spirit when we are saved makes us spiritually as fresh and pure as a newborn baby. We're correct in believing that the instant we received Jesus as Lord, our spiritual past was washed clean, our sinful history gone. But we're wrong to assume that in the same moment, our thinking, twisted by years of awful experience, was automatically untangled, and the emotional scars of our past wiped away.

That is a serious mistake.

For years after I was saved, however, I didn't know any better. Nobody made it clear to me that—unlike the rebirth of my spirit which was completed in a single moment—the renewing of my mind and the transformation of my soul (which includes the mind, will, and emotions) was a process. A process that would require my active participation. A process that God in His faithfulness would be guiding me through for the rest of my life.

If I had taken the time to fellowship with Jesus and let His truth work more deeply in me, I would have recognized my mistake and corrected it. But I didn't. So I had to learn the hard way how costly a failed journey of inches can be. I had to find out through brokenness and tears that the difference between a mental knowledge of the truth and a heart revelation of it can mean the difference between life and death.

Striving for Perfection

I marvel now that somehow I didn't see it sooner. It should have dawned on me by looking at my life that 1 Corinthians 5:17 wasn't offering all-round instant perfection. Clearly, my life wasn't perfect. Nor was I, although I almost killed myself trying to be.

Don't get me wrong, receiving Jesus as my Savior had wrought immediate and monumental changes in me. I stopped smoking pot, for example. (Good start, right?) I traded my loose-living hippie friends for a close-knit fellowship of Jesus Freaks who carried Bibles the size of Volkswagens. (What can I say? It was the '70s.) I gave up the idea of killing my mother. (Long story. More about it later.) I joined a church, married Dennis—a devoted believer with ministry in his sights—and started studying the Bible.

Granted, a few anger issues still haunted me. And some nagging insecurities. Yes, I was extra careful about keeping my house spotless and I was maniacally organized. (Can anyone say, *Obsessive Compulsive?*) Ignoring Dennis as he begged me, "Vikki, lighten up!" I approached everything from finances to ministry to planning our family vacation as if it was brain surgery. *Intense* didn't even begin to cover it.

Regardless of what Dennis said, I didn't see it as a problem. So what if I had an especially strong work ethic? Why should I apologize for that? It was a virtue, not a flaw. I didn't need to lighten up; he and everybody else in my world needed to tighten up.

In moments of brutal honesty I did have to admit, if only to myself, that now and then my tightness got out of hand—like the times in our early years of marriage when Dennis traveled out of town and I worked at the office *all night long*. But I didn't tell anybody about that. Not Dennis. Not the ministers we worked for back then. Nobody. Because I dashed home at 7 a.m. to shower and change clothes and came back at 8:30, not even the other employees knew.

It was no big deal anyway. If someone had found me out and asked why I did it, I could have easily explained. I would have said it was because there was so much to do and, after all, I didn't mind the long hours. Working made me feel good. It got my blood pumping, gave me a sense of accomplishment. What's more, I worked those hours in service to God.

That's what I would have said.

What I wouldn't have said was that working made me feel valuable. It gave me worth. It made me feel secure, and in control. I wouldn't have mentioned that because I didn't know it.

Do you know what else I wouldn't have mentioned? That I learned my work habits from my father. The son of a Mexican immigrant. A man who quit school in the eighth grade to help support his family. My father was the one who drilled into me the belief that working would get me through anything. "Work hard; harder than anyone else," he would say. "Be willing to do more than the other guy and you'll always make it."

My father's dogged determination to work was the only thing I prized about my heritage. As a kid, I loved looking at the photo of him standing proud in his black leather jacket, crisp white shirt, and blue jeans, receiving an award for excellence in aviation mechanics. Surrounded by executives dressed in expensive suits, my dad outclassed everybody else in the picture because for all their money and status, they hadn't worked half as hard as he did to get to the top of their profession.

There was just one problem. The photo didn't tell the whole story. It didn't show the alcoholism that eventually overtook my father. Or the violence that erupted between him and my mother, along with the screaming arguments and accusations, and the guns. It didn't show the neglect of family responsibilities or the cancer that, robbing my father of even his strength to work, finally ended it all.

By the time I was grown, my hatred of all those things and the shame that washed over me when I remembered them, swallowed up the glimmer of pride I once felt in my dad. The picture of him in his black leather jacket became just another picture. A piece of the past I thought I left behind forever the day I was born again.

It would never have occurred to me to tell anyone about that past after I became a Christian. I didn't even tell Dennis about it for the first 15 years we were married. I figured since old things had passed away, I didn't have to talk about them unless I wanted to. And I didn't want to because, new creature or not, whenever I remembered the life I lived before I knew Jesus, I felt so terribly ashamed.

The Girl Who Loved to Iron

It was in 1979, with all the secrets of my past still untold, that Dennis and I started our own ministry. He did all the preaching, teaching, and ministering to the people; I did everything else.

Everything.

I traveled with him so I could be in his services, sitting with open Bible on the front row, listening with rapt attention. When we weren't on the road, I became the ministry office manager, compiling mailing lists, duplicating tapes, packaging and filling product orders. If Dennis wrote a letter that needed editing, I grabbed my pencil. If we needed a brochure or catalog, I became a production coordinator, overseeing artwork, printing, and mailing. Payroll and accounting—that was me too. Have calculator, will travel.

As the ministry grew and we had to expand our computer capabilities, I researched what kind of equipment and database was needed. Waving off Dennis's suggestion to hire more help, when we forayed into publishing, I said, "No problem, I can figure it out." Newsletters? Just call me Rupert Murdock. Books? Mrs. Random House, here. It appeared there was nothing I couldn't do.

Somewhere in the midst of it all our daughter, Jessica, was born. Unwilling to cut back on my responsibilities and delegate the ministry work I'd been doing (who could I trust to do it as well?), I added the job of Super Mom to the list. We took Jessica on the road with us when we traveled. When she got old enough, I home schooled (or hotel-room-schooled) her. If Dennis traveled alone, I worked double time at home mowing grass, paying bills, running errands, and cleaning house so that when he got home, he and Jessica would have nothing to do but play together.

Dennis didn't require me to do all those things, by the way. He would have never expected it if I hadn't insisted. I was the one who named the tune. He and Jessica just played along. Who wouldn't?

As the years rushed by, it began to look like my efficiency was boundless, that my time never ran out. But there was one thing I never got around to. I couldn't make a place in my jam-packed schedule for developing relationships. Not even a relationship with God. Although I attended church services and ministry conventions and heard the Word, personal devotional time was a luxury I couldn't afford. How could I sit still to read the Bible and pray with print deadlines looming, phones ringing, and planes to catch?

I blush now to think of it, but I didn't even take a few minutes each day to ask God to help me handle those things.

It didn't seem to me that I needed any help. If I'd thought of it, I could have said, "Hey, God, don't worry about any of this stuff. I've got it handled." I didn't, though. I was too busy.

It seems absurd, doesn't it? A person in ministry focusing so much on serving God that they neglect to have a relationship with Him? But after spending years around other ministers I can tell you, it happens all the time.

I can also tell you that whether you're in ministry or not, it's a prescription for disaster.

I didn't realize it back then, of course. I was just doing the best I knew how. Repeating patterns from the past I thought I'd put behind me, I was relating to my Heavenly Father the same way I'd once related to my earthly father—by working for Him.

That's the kind of thing that happens when we settle for a superficial, head-knowledge of the truth. We repeat old patterns without even noticing. We overlook the inconsistencies between our beliefs and our behavior. Because we don't give the Holy Spirit the opportunity to help us, we fail to identify and apply the Word to mindsets we've carried over from the past.

Romans 12:2 says, "Let God transform you into a new person by changing the way you think." To obey that command, we must spend time fellowshipping with the Lord and meditating on His Word. We must let it make its journey of inches because it's not just what's recorded in our brain that makes the difference. It's the Word that is "implanted and rooted" in our hearts that has the power to save our soul (James 1:21, The Amplified Bible).

It never crossed my mind to connect my frenetic work for God with the compulsive cleaning and straightening I did as a child. I never stopped to fellowship with Him long enough to hear Him say, *Hey, Vikki. Do you remember that your favorite pastime as a girl was ironing your dad's shirts? That's a little bizarre, don't you think? A kid who loves to iron. We need to talk about that...*

It might sound strange to you, but that's the kind of conversation we all need to have with God now and then. We need to stop being so churchy in our chats with Him. We need to let Him dig around in our lives and show us why certain things aren't working. It would have helped me so much to remember the ironing. To remember that I loved it not just because I enjoyed being helpful, but because it gave me a fleeting sense of control over the chaos of my home.

Watching wrinkles disappear in the wake of steaming steel and putting a perfect crease in a collar helped me forget the overflowing trash cans and laundry baskets that spilled their contents onto the floor around me. The empty ketchup bottles nesting amid dirty socks. The cockroaches scurrying from the pockets of blue jeans and shirts left sprawled on the floor. The mouse in the cabinet gnawing the corner of the Cheerios box that held my only hope for supper.

For a moment, ironing made something perfect in my life; and ironing my father's shirts made it especially so. Phrases like *I love you* were never spoken in my family, hugs were never exchanged, so ironing was a way to show I cared. It was a way to keep the strict rule of emotional silence and say to my father without words that in spite of all the pain, I loved him.

I'd like to think the workaholic pattern that emerged years later in ministry carried the same communication. It would be nice if the first 25 years of my Christian life and ministry had some such value. But if I'm honest, I have to say that for the most part all the work I did for God and everybody else during those years was just my way of trying to prove myself.

I was "ironing" everything I could get my hands on, trying to make things around me perfect. And I did it for one primary reason: *because I felt so imperfect, so deeply flawed, myself.*

It didn't work, of course. I always ended up making a mistake or falling short in one way or another. When I did, I was devastated and I tried to make up for it by working harder...and harder...and harder.

Instead of a *human being*, I became a *human doing*. And here's the kicker: All the while, I was congratulating myself that I had beaten the statistics. I had emerged from a dysfunctional, alcoholic, abusive home unscathed. I had no addictions. No problem with drugs or alcohol. I was a good Christian with a successful ministry and an ideal family.

There was only one thing wrong with me.

Somewhere deep inside, I was very, very tired.

Sometimes people ask what pushed me over the edge. Although I can point to a particular incident, it would be wrong to blame that one thing, to say it's what shattered me into pieces. The emotional earthquake that rocked my world might not have shaken someone else's. It was simply the last straw—the one that broke the camel's back and sent it staggering to its knees.

In my life, as in the camel's, the straw wasn't the problem. The problem was the load I was already carrying—a back-breaking bundle of shame, fear, guilt, and inferiority I'd been hauling around since childhood. Burdens from the past I thought I'd left behind. Memories buried and forgotten instead of carried to Jesus and transformed by the power of His Word.

Maybe you can relate. Maybe you've been carrying a load like that yourself.

Sitting on the Edge of Eternity

The breakdown came in August 1994. I don't remember the exact day. I'm sure it was a scorcher, though, because Texas days in August always are. Television meteorologists, bored with exclaiming over today's high and inventing a hundred different ways to say *hot*, drag camera crews downtown and fry eggs on the sidewalk.

It's not one day's heat but the accumulation of weeks of it that cooks the egg. That's the way it was for me. The pressures accumulated until one day, I was fried.

Utterly spent, I fell across the bed and gave up. I had no more strength. No more desire to live. All I wanted was to die.

Impossible as it seemed, I'd come full circle. I had no idea how it had happened. After all, I was a grown up Christian woman, a new creature in Christ. Yet, as I wept into the fluffy floral comforter on our king size bed, surrounded by luxuries I couldn't have dreamed of as a child, I felt the same desperation that once gripped me as a spiritually lost nine-year-old girl sobbing in the grass behind my parents' house.

Then, as now, I had begged God to kill me. Lifting my arms to heaven with tears streaming down my face, I could think of no other way out of the pain. I'd watched my older sisters try to escape my mother's rage, my father's alcoholism, and the abuse that followed, by running away. But the police brought them back. That was in the days before Child Protective Services. When children ran away they were returned, despite purple bruises and fear-stricken eyes, to their abusive parents.

My nine-year-old mind reckoned that I wouldn't be free or safe until I walked away from my childhood home legally at 18 years old. Another nine years was a lifetime to me. I'd rather die than wait that long.

In my family's rare visits to the Catholic church, I'd learned just enough to be sure of two things. First, reading the Bible would drive you insane. Second, suicide sentenced you to hell with no exceptions. Trading nine years of hell for an eternity of it didn't make sense, so I begged for some benevolent divine hand to blot me out.

I have no idea why, but my mother was playing spiritual music on her record player that day. The melody wafting through her open window on the warm southern California wind carried the words of the old Stuart Hamlin song, "It Is No Secret What God Can Do." Hoping the God of that song would hear me, I asked Him to take my life.

Now decades later, I was beseeching Him to do me the same favor. This time, however, I knew more about Him. I knew that reading the Bible wouldn't drive me crazy. I knew that because I'd received Jesus as my Savior, death was the only thing standing between me and an eternity in heaven. I knew the sin of suicide wouldn't send me to hell.

I also knew that, no matter how I begged Him, He would not kill me. I would have to do the job myself.

My tears spent, I wiped my eyes and sat for a while, slumped and motionless, on the edge of the bed. Beside me on the nightstand, a white porcelain clock painted with delicate flowers sounded out the seconds. I listened to the soft *tick...tick...tick* as I dangled my feet over the edge of eternity, wondering whether to jump in. God knows, it's what I wanted. I was too exhausted to do anything else and too disappointed in myself and everyone else to hope that things would ever change. I'd given life my best shot...and failed.

Death would be a blessing to me now. Only one thought kept me from embracing it without reserve. Jessica. What about Jessica? I understood what it meant to lose a parent. My father's death from cancer when I was 16 had wrenched my heart and left me burning with anger, not at my dad but at God. Could I risk putting my daughter through the same experience—not by cancer but by choice?

No. I couldn't. I wouldn't. I had to fight the desire to die if only for her sake.

I needed help but had no idea who to call. I had no close friends. None of the ministers I knew had ever faced anything like this. Most of us were baffled by terms like *burnout* or *breakdown*. Never having been there, I suppose, we assumed people who suffered something like that should simply get up and get over it.

We would never have taken such a calloused attitude toward someone suffering a physical illness or injury. We wouldn't have ordered a person with cancer to simply forget it and go on. That would be cruel; and we weren't cruel people. We just didn't understand that wounded emotions and crippled souls require the same kind of healing power and process that wounded or crippled bodies require.

With nowhere to turn, I struggled alone to regain my will to live. Days crept into weeks, then weeks into months as I pushed myself, zombielike, through the motions of living. Staying in bed and pulling the covers over my head was not an option. Neither was checking myself into a hospital, though it would have been wise. I was convinced that if anyone found out what I was going through, it would ruin our ministry. We'd be judged and rejected. Criticized and cast aside. My peers would see all this as unacceptable, of that I was sure.

Stiffening myself against the pain, I kept up appearances, acted the part. I got up and got dressed every morning. Made the bed. Arranged the throw pillows and opened the bedroom blinds. I made coffee. Drove to the office. Came home and cooked dinner. Cried myself to sleep, woke up the next morning and started over again.

Dennis and Jessica tiptoed around me in silence for the most part. They had no idea what to do or how to help. Outside, sun-baked August days mellowed into a soft Indian summer. September swept in with the reminder that even in Texas, autumn eventually arrives. On the street, fresh scrubbed yellow buses packed with children huffed and screaked. In the sky, the sun slipped a little, lengthening the shadows, but not enough to dim the seasonal optimism of southerners in the fall.

I know these things happened, not because I noticed them, but because they happen every year. Sunk down in a chasm of despair, I was blind to them all. The sun might just as well have gone dark altogether as far as I was concerned.

The only bright spot in my day was when—having shuttered my mind against thoughts of suicide—I dreamed of simply running away. Of packing a single suitcase and driving to a dusty little town where nobody knew me. Of getting a job pouring coffee into chipped ceramic mugs for leathery-skinned ranchers, sleepy-eyed truckers, and clerks wearing plastic nametags from the Tack and Feed or the Sears Catalog Store.

It was ridiculous, I know, but the way I imagined it, such people were happy and carefree. They chatted about the norther that blew in last night or how the high school quarterback might take the team to state this year. And all they required from me was to ask questions like, "What'll you have today?" and to scribble phrases like *meatloaf w/ mashed potato* onto palm-sized pieces of paper.

Such were the pictures floating through my mind one day in early October when a single horrifying thought slapped me back to reality. Dennis and I were scheduled to teach a marriage seminar. At a large church. At the end of the month.

Panicked, I shuffled through the papers on my desk and checked my calendar. There it was. *Marriage Seminar.* A wave of nausea swept over me. Oh, dear God, no. There's no way. How could I possibly do it?

On my best days, I struggled with public speaking. In school, I detested it so much that even if it cost me a grade, I refused. Teachers could cajole and threaten all they wanted; I would not talk in front of a group. Period. End of discussion. Over the years, I had softened my stance a bit. For Jesus and for the ministry, I agreed to speak on occasion in church meetings of various sorts but I was still uncomfortable with it.

What's worse, I was a complete wreck. Even if I could think of something to say, even if I found a way to force myself through it, I would feel so phony. What kind of hypocrite quotes scriptures about marriage to other people when for the past two months, she's gone to sleep every night on a tear-wilted pillow, longing to leave not just her husband, but her whole life?

It was too late to cancel the seminar. Announcements had been made. People had made plans. The pastors of the church would be embarrassed and disappointed. Dennis would look foolish. What excuse would he give? He'd either have to lie or make public the fact that his wife had lost her mind, her heart, and her will to live.

Somewhere in the office a phone rang and someone answered in muffled tones that sounded a thousand miles away. A file drawer clanged shut from the same distance. Fluorescent lights glared overhead as darkness fell inside me. Images of running away, of coffee cups and carefree conversations, vanished, giving way again to thoughts of death. I was so tired of performing. So tired of trying and failing to be perfect. So weary of working and working and working to please everyone—including God. I just wanted it all to be over. I wanted to go to heaven.

White-knuckled, I gripped the padded arms of the desk chair, as if to anchor myself to the earth. Then, realizing I had no desire to hold on anymore, I leaned back, closed my eyes and let go. Jarred loose from my fragile attachment to the planet, my heart drifted away, drawn by the massive gravitational pull of a more celestial place.

Heaven.

As a believer, I knew it was just a heartbeat away. I understood, with dangerous clarity, that those who arrive there, "...shall neither hunger anymore nor thirst anymore; the sun shall not strike them, nor any heat; for the Lamb who is in the midst of the throne will shepherd them and lead them to living fountains of waters. And God will wipe away every tear from their eyes" (Revelation 7:16-17).

This nightmare could all be over so quickly.

But, Jessica.

Dennis could go on. He would be okay.

But, Jessica...

I don't have much in common with the apostle Paul. My suffering, unlike his, was not persecution for Christ's sake. It was due, not to my great revelation, but to my lack of it. Yet at that moment, I could have spoken with all honesty the words he wrote to the Philippians from a Roman prison. Clinging to life while longing for death I could have said, "...I am hard pressed between the two, having a desire to depart and be with Christ, which is far better. Nevertheless to remain in the flesh is more needful for you" (Philippians 1:23-24).

Jessica.

Jaw locked, I made up my mind to find a way to "remain in the flesh."

In the days that followed, it became clear I was too weak, too confused, to find it on my own. I had to have a human hand to guide me. A human voice to speak to me. I needed what we all need at times, even though we like to pretend that we don't. I needed, as some people say, *God with skin on.*

Alone at home, I picked up the phone and called a ministry I thought might be able to help. It was hundreds of miles away in another state. I had no personal relationship with anyone there. No idea who to ask for when a brisk voice answered, "Focus on the Family. How can I help you?"

Pressing the phone hard to my ear, I felt the tears trace their familiar path down my cheeks as I spoke my shameful secret to a total stranger.

"I'm in trouble...and I need to talk to a counselor."

CHAPTER 3

The Offer I Couldn't Refuse

*Come into fellowship with me if you are tired and
burdened, and I will refresh and release you. Take the
burden of responsibility I give you and thereby discover
your life and your destiny. I am gentle and humble; I
am willing to relate to you and to permit you to learn
at your own rate; then, in fellowship with me, you will
discover the meaning of your life. My fellowship will
release you, and my companionship will direct you on
your journey.*

Matthew 11:28-30
Ben Campbell Johnson Paraphrase

Except for the flair of its French-style roof, the single
story brown brick office building looked as ordinary
as a loaf of bread. But for me, there was nothing ordinary
about this day. Nothing normal about walking into a counselor's office.

Drawing a deep breath, I dropped my car keys into my
purse, squared my shoulders, and prepared myself to go
inside.

This had not been a hasty decision. After my initial call to
Focus on the Family, I'd interviewed a number of counselors

looking for one I felt I could trust. Still unsure if I even believed in counseling, I didn't want to risk getting tangled up in a process that would leave me worse instead of better. So I'd set up strict and specific guidelines.

I considered only counselors who shared my faith in God, for instance. If they didn't use the Bible as their standard of truth, they couldn't help me. Of that I was sure. I also decided I didn't want to talk to a man, or anyone critical of my position in ministry. One candidate reacted to my situation with a kind of judgmental horror. "...And you are a *minister!*" she exclaimed. I didn't need any additional condemnation; I had plenty of it on my own so I crossed her off the list.

In the end, I'd settled on this place because one of the counselors here, a woman named Ava, had once been a Bible school teacher at a church I respected. She was a strong woman of the Word with a prophetic gift and a kind, gentle temperament.

When we talked on the phone, she'd seemed wonderful. I'd been certain she was the right choice. But now, when I needed it most, my certainty was gone. Dread dogged my steps as I made my way through the silent reception area toward her office. Heart skittering, I looked down the hall. Three doors. Two of them closed. I imagined people—*Patients? Clients? What's the right term?*—pouring out problems to spectacle-wearing, note-taking therapists.

Ridiculous thoughts. Good thing counselors aren't mind readers.

"Hello, you must be Vikki. I'm Ava."

Smiling and extending her hand, she didn't look at all (*of course*) like the therapists I'd imagined. No spectacles perched on her nose or dangled from a chain around her neck. What I noticed instead was a chunky bracelet, matching earrings, and a stylish fluff of brown hair.

She ushered me into a room that looked more like a living room than an office. No desk in sight, two wingback chairs arranged across from a small sofa invited conversation. Instead of overhead lighting, lamps cast a cozy glow. On the walls, pictures added warmth and color.

I should have felt at home right away, but I didn't.

Sitting on the sofa, rigid and on guard like a child in a dentist's chair, I clasped my hands in my lap and waited wordlessly for whatever came next. We had discussed my general situation a few days earlier when we talked on the phone. What else was I supposed to say?

Ava settled herself across from me in one of the chairs. After a few pleasantries meant to put me at ease (*Right. Like that was going to happen.*) she began with a brief review of our phone conversation. Then she went straight to the heart of the matter.

"Vikki, tell me about your relationship with your mother," she said.

A cold, familiar surge of anger shot through me. Ice water in my veins. It was the worst question she could have asked me...and the most stupid. As far as I was concerned, my mother was not an issue. Yes, there had been a time when my relationship with her had been a problem. To be blunt, there was a time when I hated her. A time when, after enduring years of abuse, something in me snapped and I wanted—and even tried—to kill her.

But that was before I gave my life to Jesus. It was before I made the decision to forgive her, before the Holy Spirit taught me to stop spewing bitterness and start confessing that I love her. It had been years since I'd put behind me all the pain and ugliness of my childhood. I saw no point in going over it again. My mother was ancient history.

Ava leaned back in her chair, the picture of patience, and waited for my answer. She wanted to help me; that was clear. I should at least give her a chance. Hearing in my voice the steely edge of a kid who'd become tough as nails just to survive, I responded with a question of my own.

"What does my mother have to do with this?" I asked.

"Everything," Ava answered.

God Said It First

It seems so obvious I'm almost embarrassed to say it, yet I've come to realize over the years that this needs to be said: Psychologists weren't the first ones to tell us that parents are important. The idea that our fathers and mothers shaped our thoughts and perceptions in ways so powerful that they've affected our entire lives didn't originate with counselors and therapists. It started with God. He was the first One to tell parents about their crucial role in the lives of their children. He is the One who first revealed how vital it is for moms and dads to teach their sons and daughters His Word and His ways. Over and over, in the Bible, He gives instructions like these:

- …lay up these words of mine in your heart and in your soul, and…teach them to your children, speaking of them when you sit in your house, when you walk by the way, when you lie down, and when you rise up… (Deuteronomy 11:18-19).

- …. take heed to yourself, and diligently keep yourself, lest you forget the things your eyes have seen, and lest they depart from your heart all the days of your life. And teach them to your children and your grandchildren... (Deuteronomy 4:9).

- Train up a child in the way he should go, and when he is old he will not depart from it (Proverbs 22:6).

- ....do not provoke your children to wrath, but bring them up in the training and admonition of the Lord (Ephesians 6:4).

God doesn't waste words in Scripture. If He takes the time to hammer home a point in verse after verse, it's because so much depends on it. This is no exception. God knew long before we did just how much difference parents can make. He understood, far better than any psychoanalyst ever will, that children get the first glimpse of their own value—or lack of it—by looking in the mirror of their parents' eyes.

In the mind and heart of a child, if his parents love and prize him, he is lovable and precious. If they don't, he is not. Even before he has words to explain it, a child finds his identity in his mother and father's estimation of him. He patterns all other relationships, including his relationship with God, after that first vital relationship with his parents.

As Christians, you and I know that God can change those initial patterns. His redemptive truth is plenty powerful enough to remedy all that inevitably goes wrong in this fallen world during the first tender years of childhood. But His Word works only when the need for it is identified and the remedy applied as prescribed.

There's where I went wrong. For years I had carried my Bible around like a bottle full of a magnificent medicine. Now and again I pulled off the cap, admired the contents, and took a bit of it for the sake of my general spiritual health.

I even testified to people about how it had changed my life. But I neglected to apply it specifically to the problems I was experiencing because, until I totally fell apart, I didn't acknowledge them.

Now those problems could no longer be denied. They had forced me into a counselor's office and I was being asked to consider that whatever it was that was wrong with me might have something to do with my childhood.

Ava's words hung in the air, inescapable. *Tell me about your mother.*

"Okay…" I said.

The words began to flow—first in a trickle then in a torrent—as I talked about how, for as long as I could remember, I struggled to please my mother to no avail. How she often responded to my efforts by shaking her head and saying, "I should have never had children." I described the years of neglect and abuse, the filthy house that made me so ashamed that I refused to allow my friends inside, and my compulsive cleaning that made so little difference. I recalled a time when I spent hours scrubbing the kitchen floor and my brother ruined it by tromping through with muddy feet. My mother—inexplicably annoyed not with my brother but with me—had cut short my tears of dismay. "Oh, shut up!" she said as she turned away from me in disgust.

Thinking back on it all, I wondered aloud about why, in spite of my mother's relentless rebuffs, I never stopped trying to win her approval. When she dropped me off as a trembling 13-year-old at Lucky's Grocery store to do the family shopping, I never thought of objecting or asking for help. I simply watched mute with fear as my mother's Lincoln Continental disappeared around the corner of Crenshaw Street onto Torrance Boulevard. White knuckled, I gripped the two crinkled

$20 bills she had stuffed into my hand and resolved once again to do my best.

Telling Ava the story, I could almost hear the wobbly-wheeled cart clattering as I pushed it up and down the aisles, trying with all my might to figure out how to buy a week's worth of groceries for a family of four for less than $40. I broke out in a cold sweat at the checkout stand worrying if I'd have enough to pay the bill. Afterward, I'd waited an hour outside under eucalyptus trees in front of Lucky's with my full shopping cart. My mother eventually came back for me, but if I hoped she'd say *Thank you*, or *Good job*, I was disappointed. She never did.

I didn't cry about these things as I described them to Ava. They were old wounds to me. Scarred over and without feeling.

Shaking my head at the absurdity of it, I remembered how my mother seemed to resent even my hair. How she once got so fed up with the way it hung straight and limp around my face that she decided—come hell or high water—she was going to style it. The problem was, no matter what she did, it kept falling back into place. Every time it fell, she raised her hand in fury and slapped me...again...and again...and again.

Somehow in her eyes, and therefore in mine, even the unacceptable way my hair grew was my fault. Long after the slapping had stopped and the throbbing in my face subsided, my heart continued to ache. It took me hours that day to stifle my sobs.

Tears glistened in Ava's eyes as she listened. Glancing up in surprise, I asked her what was the matter.

"I just can't imagine how awful that would be," she said. "My mother is my best friend."

The thought pierced my soul like a lance through a boil but I responded with chilled matter-of-factness. "I'd rather not talk about your mother if it's all the same to you."

Useful Enough to Be Loved

Ava wasn't offended, of course. She understood far better than I did what was happening. A pattern was emerging. She had already identified it. I, however, had not, so she encouraged me to continue. Asking me about my father, she listened, intent and patient, as I told her that when I was 15 and my father was dying of cancer, I had taken over his care. My mother could no longer stay with him because she had to work.

A terrified teenager without a driver's license, I braved the hair-raising highways of Los Angeles all by myself to deliver him to the medical clinic for his cobalt treatments. Dad hated being dependent on me but he had no choice. The day he handed me the keys to his copper colored El Camino—his pride and joy—he did it with excruciating reluctance. "You aren't insured, Vikki, so if you have a wreck it will wipe us out," he said. Then he crawled into the passenger seat and, pillowing his head on his arm, he closed his eyes and got on with the business of dying.

It might have been then—telling Ava how I ran to my father's bedside in the days before his death to answer his every call—that I began to see the pattern. Ever since I could remember, I'd worked hard and taken on ever increasing loads of responsibility in a desperate attempt to earn my parents' love. Sensing how much of a disappointment I was to them, I struggled to make up for it by being...*useful*.

All the way to the end, I'd hoped that if I was useful enough, if I did everything my dad needed me to do, I would finally hear him say, "I love you." It almost happened, I think. A few days before he died, he called me into his room, stretched his hands out to me and said with an earnestness I'd never before heard in his voice, "Vikki, I want you to know...I don't hate Diablo. I don't hate him. I need you to know that."

Diablo?

Diablo was my horse—the only gift I could remember ever asking for and receiving from my parents. I loved him dearly and my father knew it. When I took on the responsibility of caring for Dad, I kept Diablo in the yard behind the house rather than at the stable so I could look after them both. Time and again, Dad had railed about the mess the horse made of the lawn and declared his hatred for him.

Now he wanted me to know that he didn't really hate Diablo? I stood a few feet from my father's outstretched hands, frozen with confusion at his awkward deathbed confession. Surely, there was something more he wanted to say. Something about me...

Whatever it was—if it was—he never said it.

Instead, he waved me away in anger. Garnering his strength, he spat the words with all the force he could muster. "Get out of here, Vikki. Just get out!"

Some time not long afterward, he died. Within weeks, my mother had moved another man into the house to take his place.

Outside Ava's office I heard the click of a door being opened somewhere. Muffled voices drifted down the hall toward the reception area. Someone's session was over.

Glancing at my watch, I saw that in a few minutes mine would be too.

"Well, that's enough about the past," I said, shooing it away with a wave of my hand. "I decided long ago that my parents had their own hurts and struggles. I love them and I've forgiven them. They did the best they knew how. It's all over now. I've moved on."

Have you? I could see the question in her eyes.

At the time, it irritated me. But I know now how vital that question is, not just for me but for you and every other Christian who wants to regain their lost freedom. We must all ask ourselves and our God if we've really gotten over the pain of the past...or if we're ignoring it, like the proverbial 800 pound gorilla, while living in its shadow.

Not yet ready to answer such a question, I brushed it aside and I took my conversation with Ava in another direction. "What I need most today is help with my present situation," I said. "To be specific, the marriage seminar that Dennis and I are scheduled to lead—I absolutely cannot face it."

If I mentioned suicide, Ava would be legally bound to report it to the authorities so I avoided the word with care. I described instead the weariness and the dread that mounted with every passing day. "It's pushing me to an end," I said.

I had no idea what I needed Ava to tell me at that moment. I couldn't think of a single thing that I wanted to hear. But by the grace of God, she found the perfect words. They wrapped around me, strong arms around a sinking soul, and for the first time in months I entertained the hope that I would not go under, that I would somehow make it to shore.

"The Holy Spirit will help you get through," she said. "And if you will commit yourself to the process, I can help you. There's light on the other side of this darkness, Vikki. You can get free."

Just in case you're wondering, those words are as true for you as they were for me. No matter what you may be facing right now, there's light on the other side and Jesus will help you find it. No matter how imprisoned you may feel, you too can get free.

Strapped to the Rock

It's amazing how the Holy Spirit works. How He quickens a fragment of Scripture, a passing phrase of encouragement, or a story from years gone by, and turns it into a lifeline in times of crisis. For me, He used the story of the mountain climber. I heard Oral Roberts tell it once in a sermon, and during the first dark months of my journey, the Lord spoke to me through it every day.

The story is a kind of parable, really, about a climber who spends the day scaling the summit of a mountain. He reaches the peak and after taking time to enjoy the view, he begins his descent. Part way down the mountain, the climber realizes that the sun has outpaced him. Night is nipping at his heels and about to swallow him up. Terrain easily conquered in daylight can be deadly in the dark and the climber knows it. If he wants to make it home alive, there is only one thing to do.

Pulling a length of rope from his backpack, he cinches it around him, ties it around a pillar of rock, and sits down to wait out the night. No matter that the cold numbs his fingers and sends shivers through his bones. No matter that pebbles pock his backside and sleep stays away. "What matters," he says to himself aloud, "is that I don't plummet to my death in the darkness. What matters is that when morning comes, I'm still here."

During my blackest moments, when even my will to pray or read the Bible fled from me, I was often reminded of the mountain climber's wisdom. When, in the midst of pain and panic, I was tempted to make rash decisions, to do something to end it all, the Holy Spirit brought to my mind Brother Roberts' words: "In our darkest moment, when the sun sets and night falls, when we cannot see and we feel afraid, there is one thing we must do. We must strap ourselves to God. He is our Rock. In Him, we trust."

For several weeks, it was the only thing I knew to do. So, sitting down in the chair in my bedroom, I strapped my heart to the Rock, and waited day after day after day for morning to come.

It's proof of the goodness of God that He didn't give up on me during those days. I certainly gave Him reason enough. Even as I waited on Him for help, my anger erupted in ways that would be—to put it mildly—unacceptable in church. Furious and depressed, I refused to put a nice Christian face on my feelings. This was the reality: I was mad at everybody, God included. Mad that after working so hard and sacrificing so much—for God, for Dennis, for Jessica, and everybody else—my life had collapsed into a burnt out, broken down pile of rubble.

I don't recommend this, but it's the truth. Some days I literally shook my fist at God and said, "If You can't get me through this mess, You're not big enough to be my God."

On the surface, it sounds like an insolent prayer best answered by a lightning bolt of divine wrath. Or, at the very least, a cold shoulder. But God overlooked my religious impropriety and responded in a way that confirmed the truth of Psalm 145:8-9,

> *The LORD is gracious and full of compassion, slow to anger and great in mercy. The LORD is good to all, and His tender mercies are over all His works.*

Truly, Jesus is wonderful. He can and will do for us what no one else ever would. He proved it to me the day He reached down into the pit I'd fallen into and started pulling me out with words so clear and simple that I couldn't miss their meaning. I didn't hear them with my physical ears. But inside me they rang out loud as church bells.

Maybe that's because I'd been sitting for so many days in silence. Normal family conversations had all but ceased at our house. Dennis, sensing my anger and having no idea how to quell it, went about his daily tasks without comment. When he was home, he kept a wary distance, like a man trying to live with a polecat. When he was gone, which was often, the quiet in the house was absolute.

The one major decision I'd allowed myself to make was to enroll Jessica in Christian school, so there were no papers rattling or books thumping shut in the daytime as there had been in days past. No ice rattled in glasses and no plates clattered at lunch time. Sitting alone in the bedroom, looking out the window at the cluster of oak trees in the backyard, the only sound I heard was a rare bark from our neighbor's Rottweiler.

It was in the midst of this deafening silence that God spoke and I heard Him.

To say it that way sounds monumental, I realize, but to an onlooker it wouldn't have seemed so at all. No cloud of glory descended. No voice boomed from the heavens. If you'd been there, all you would have seen was me sitting in my familiar place reading the only book I could manage—a paraphrase of the New Testament by Ben Campbell Johnson.

I'd given up trying to read the more traditional translations of the Bible. Somehow in my muddled condition, they just didn't speak to me anymore. The Johnson paraphrase used words that jarred me out of my spiritual coma, unexpected phrases that cut through the fog. And on the day things began to change, they did even more than that. They rose up from the page by the power of the Holy Spirit and became the most personal message from God I had ever received.

Come into fellowship with me if you are tired and burdened, and I will refresh and release you. Take the burden of responsibility I give you and thereby discover your life and your destiny. I am gentle and humble; I am willing to relate to you and to permit you to learn at your own rate; then, in fellowship with me, you will discover the meaning of life. My fellowship will release you, and my companionship will direct you on your journey.

Matthew 11:28-30 BCJ

Astonished, I fixed my eyes on the words as though they would vanish if I looked away. They seemed too good to be true. Hardly daring to believe them, I wanted to be sure I understood.

"Jesus," I said, "would You really do that for me? Would You really permit me to learn at my own rate? To progress at my own pace? I'm in a major deficit here. I can't move very fast. I can't do much. Sometimes I can't even read the Bible. This is going to be a slow journey if You permit me to set the speed. Are You really willing to do that?"

His answer was tender and clear in my spirit. "Yes, I am with you. If you'll come with Me, I will lead you forward at your own pace. No matter how long it takes, I'll direct you all the way and help you find a life that is so meaningful, so full of joy, so refreshing, that you won't recognize it."

Lifting my eyes from the page, I gazed out the window. Outside in the yard, the white nylon hammock that stretched from one oak to another swayed gently in the breeze. A few feet beyond it, the creek that bordered our property swished and glittered in the sun. For the first time it seemed that what they represented just might be within my reach. *Rest. Refreshing. A life like I'd never known before.*

Jesus was offering it to me and I was taking Him up on it.

One way or another, things would never be the same again.

Clearing Away the Rubble

I wonder sometimes if the Old Testament wall-builder, Nehemiah, had a clue what he was taking on when he left the king's palace in Persia and headed for Jerusalem to rebuild the city. Did he imagine he'd ride in with his carpenters and contractors and start making great progress right away? Or did he realize that he'd first have to get rid of massive piles of burned out, broken down rubble?

Either way, I appreciate him. I'm glad that he provided an example of someone who faced "so much rubble" that it had to be moved before construction could begin (Nehemiah 4:10). In the first months of my journey to freedom, I needed that example. I found out right quick, just as Nehemiah did, that when it comes to rebuilding, clearing away the rubble is often the first—and the hardest—thing you have to do.

The phrase from Matthew 11, "Take the burden of responsibility I give you...," is what started the process. As I meditated on it, the Holy Spirit emphasized to me the importance of taking on *ONLY* the responsibilities God gave me and no others. I saw that in seeking God's purpose and destiny for my life, the first thing I must do is get rid of all the things I had added on myself.

Add-ons. That's what I called them. Like Nehemiah's rubble, they had cluttered up my life for years, sapping my strength, stopping me from doing what God specifically called me to do.

I understood from my first sessions with Ava why I'd accumulated so many of them. I was trying to earn love by my behavior and performance. I was trying to prove my worth by being useful—not only to other people but to God. Given the mindsets and patterns developed in my childhood, it's easy to see why I did it. But that doesn't make it okay. It doesn't change the fact that I'd spent my first 25 years as a Christian living crosswise of the most basic truth of the gospel which is this:

> *You have this new relationship with God simply by accepting it. It is his gift to you through his unconditional love. It is not something you could ever earn by any effort of your own, so you can't brag about having it, or about doing anything.*
>
> Ephesians 2:8, BCJ

For me, this was the most devastating realization: I'd wasted a quarter century of Christian service. I'd done everything for the wrong reasons. Instead of receiving by faith the love and favor of the Lord and simply doing what He directed me to do, I'd worked myself almost to death building a worthless pile of wood, hay, and stubble. (See 1 Corinthians 3:10-15.)

The fact that most other Christians, at some time in their life, have done the same thing was small comfort to me. Even though the mistake I made was a common one, I wanted someone else to blame for it. I knew, however, that passing the buck wasn't a luxury I could afford. If I was ever going to get the rubble cleared away, the first tool I had to pick up was the shovel of personal responsibility.

As a full grown, born-again child of God, I was no victim. No one else was at fault for the mess I'd gotten into. Yes, I'd been hurt and felt betrayed by people. Yes, there were others involved in the emotional storm that had whipped through my life in recent months. But it wasn't anyone else's fault that when the storm came, I lacked the spiritual strength to withstand it.

Jesus said:

"Whoever comes to Me, and hears My sayings and does them, I will show you whom he is like: He is like a man building a house, who dug deep and laid the foundation on the rock. And when the flood arose, the stream beat vehemently against that house, and could not shake it, for it was founded on the rock."

Luke 6:47-48

For far too long, I'd left my Bible lying unopened on my nightstand as I rushed off in the morning too busy to read it or fellowship with its Author. My schedule packed with the work of ministry, I hadn't taken time to dig down deep, to examine the patterns of my life in the light of the Word and make sure they were firmly founded on the Rock. I could have but I didn't. The blame game wasn't an option. If I tried to play it, I'd be stuck in the rubble for the rest of my life.

Enter: Sanballat and Associates

It was clear what had to be done. So, like Nehemiah and his crew, I rolled up my sleeves and started hauling away the junk. I spent time with the Lord in the Word and in prayer every day asking Him to show me what add-ons needed to go. Then I set out to communicate in a clear and definite way to the people around me what I would and would not be doing.

Sensing I should start on the home front, we called a family meeting and divided up the domestic responsibilities. Jessica took on the dusting, vacuuming, and some other household chores. Dennis took over our personal finances and hired someone to do the yard work.

Next I focused on the office. At the prompting of the Lord, I began delegating to ministry employees one area of responsibility after another. To say it was difficult is an understatement. Torturous is more like it. Bamboo shoots under finger nails. On the outside I kept a stiff upper lip. Inside I was screaming.

My entire life had revolved around what I accomplished—especially in ministry. My work was my identity. I'd so poured myself into building the various departments of our ministry that letting go of them was like losing a part of me. Those departments were my *babies*. How could I leave them on someone's doorstep and walk away? It felt like borderline insanity. Yet that's what the Lord was instructing me to do.

Handing off household chores had been a relief because those things weren't crucial to my self-worth. Giving up my work at the office left an almost overwhelming void in my life. Without the adrenaline rush of accomplishing an impossible number of tasks each day, I might as well have been a junkie going through withdrawal. For years, my high had come from feeling indispensible to and needed by those around me, now feeling empty and purposeless, I crashed.

To make things worse, I traded my position as the hero on the white horse for the role of wicked witch of the West. My family members, friends, and co-workers were almost as addicted to my workaholic, performance-driven lifestyle as I was. They'd become dependent on my seemingly boundless ability to help them in every way they might need it. (*In a bind? Never fear, Vikki's here!*) Once I relinquished my job as rescuer, I seemed to be always letting them down.

Even at church, I felt I was disappointing people. When asked to represent the Christian home schooling community on a new city-wide committee, for example, I declined. Although it would have nourished my aching ego and given me a workaholic fix, I knew that accepting the invitation would be a major detour from the path the Lord had laid out for me. So I thanked my fellow church member for her confidence in me and told her it wasn't something I was called to do. Then—to make us both feel better and because I believed it—I assured her that God had called someone to take the position. If I accepted it, I would prevent the right person from taking their God-given place.

Turning down that add-on was a shining moment for me. Others were not as shiny. Sometimes I fell back into my old ways and said yes to things I shouldn't. But the more I committed myself to take on only the responsibilities Jesus gave me, the more I developed my ability to say *no*.

Rather than rejoicing with me over that ability, for the most part people were annoyed by it. My rubble removal upset the balance of their lives. It made them uncomfortable and they protested in various ways. But, as Ava often reminded me, I couldn't point the finger of blame. By rescuing everyone around me, I had set up this system. I had prevented people from being responsible for themselves by doing everything for them. What I had to do now was take full responsibility for my wrongdoing and allow them to be responsible for their own issues.

If it sounds easy, I want to assure you, it wasn't.

I don't say that to discourage you. I just want you to know that if you tend to be a people-pleaser like I was, getting rid of add-ons can be an uphill battle. Not only do those around you chafe against the changes you're making, the devil also gets in on the act.

I found that out very fast. As soon as I started stepping into the liberty Jesus offered, the devil went on the attack and I found myself identifying once again with Nehemiah and the wall-builders. Like me, they didn't have the luxury of doing their work unhindered. They had enemies—

> *And it happened, when Sanballat, Tobiah, the Arabs, the Ammonites, and the Ashdodites heard that the walls of Jerusalem were being restored and the gaps were beginning to be closed, that they became very angry, and all of them conspired together to come and attack Jerusalem and create confusion...So it was, from that time on, that...those who built on the wall, and those who carried burdens, loaded themselves so that with one hand they worked at construction, and with the other held a weapon.*
>
> Nehemiah 4:7-8, 16, 17

This is something you'll want to remember as you fight the battle for your freedom: The Sanballats and associates in your life aren't people. Our enemies aren't the dear ones around us who are struggling to adjust to all the changes we're making. The New Testament makes it clear that "we

68

do not wrestle against flesh and blood, but against principalities, against powers, against the rulers of the darkness of this age, against spiritual hosts of wickedness in the heavenly places" (Ephesians 6:12).

Our Sanballats are the devilish spirits. In my case, they attacked with guilt and condemned me for ridding myself of the responsibilities God had not given me. Pointing out the discomfort my family and friends were going through, the devil told me it was all my fault. He accused me of being a bad Christian, a lousy wife, a failure as a mother, and a disgrace as a minister.

I soon learned to build, as you will, with a trowel in one hand and a weapon in the other.

CHAPTER 4

Love Letters in the Sand

*And God saw every thing that he had made, and,
behold, it was very good.*

Genesis 1:31

When Jessica was six or seven years old, I decided to buy her a puppy. To this day, I can hardly believe I did it. What was I thinking? We traveled all the time. What would we do with a puppy on the road?

It's not as if Jessica had been begging for a dog. She had never—not once—asked for one. As far as I know, she'd indicated no interest in pets at all. For some strange reason, however, none of that mattered to me. Brushing aside all sound logic and assuming that every normal child wants a puppy, I gave one to Jessica as a surprise.

I expected it to be this great, storybook kind of moment. Sneaking the dog into the house while Jessica was at the neighbor's, I met her at the door when she returned. "Close your eyes. I have a present for you!" I said.

Smiling in anticipation, she squeezed her eyelids together and held out her tiny hands.

"Ta-da!" I cried in triumph.

As her eyes popped open, Jessica's smile, rather than grow wider, collapsed. She stared down at the puppy with a kind of confused disappointment, as if I had given her something totally inappropriate, like a carburetor or vacuum cleaner bag. Talk about a letdown! None of us seemed to know what to do. Including the puppy. Expending every iota of its canine cuteness, it leapt and licked and wriggled. It rolled over and laid on its back hoping for a belly rub. But all to no avail.

Jessica simply stood there, a statue of shock.

"It's a puppy!" I said—as if she might have gone temporarily blind—"Your very own dog!"

No response. Just more stunned silence. Finally, she reached down and gave the puppy an awkward pat.

I didn't know about add-ons back then. But if I had, it might have dawned on me that I was adding onto Jessica a responsibility she didn't want. I might have realized that this waggling bundle of fur was my idea, not hers.

As it was, it didn't occur to me. Instead I wondered what on earth was wrong with her and figured that whatever it was, eventually she would get over it. Even if she didn't, I reasoned, a pet would be good for her. It would help her learn to take care of something. It would help her grow up.

Jessica was still standing dumbstruck and unsmiling when I launched into the litany of her new responsibilities. "From now on, everyday you'll have to feed the dog," I informed her. "You'll have to take it outside, keep its water bowl full, take it for walks and play with it."

Jessica's small shoulders sagged under the weight of her new chores. But there was no point in her saying anything. Apparently, her future had been decided and it included this dog.

For the first few days, things went fine. Jessica did her duty and the puppy project seemed to be a success. Then one day, she and I were in the car running some errands and I reminded her that when we got home she had work to do. "Before you play, be sure to take the dog outside," I said, "and take some time to run him around so he can get some exercise."

Jessica, sitting behind me in her little car seat (that's how young she was!), heaved a weary sigh. "I want my old life back!" she said.

I want my old life back.

Some years later, I found out just how profound that statement was. As I began to identify and eradicate the add-ons in my life, I began to realize that I, too, wanted my life back. I wanted to experience the life Jesus had destined for me.

Clearly, the add-ons had robbed me of it. They'd deprived me of the blessed yoke of Jesus that is easy and light, and replaced it with burdens too hard and heavy to bear. They'd stripped the smile off my face and left me staring bewildered at my life, like Jessica at the puppy, wondering, *Who am I? What am I doing and why am I doing it?*

Jesus, however, had offered me a way out. He'd given me an option that I didn't offer to my daughter the day I gave her the dog. He gave me permission to say no to the add-ons.

He didn't give it just to me, either. He's given it to every believer. The good news of Matthew 11:29-30 is yours just as surely as it's mine. Maybe that's obvious. But then again, maybe not. So I want to make it extra clear that my case is not unique. The Lord didn't do something special for me just because I went through tough times and had a meltdown.

He offers to everybody what He offered me—a life of rest and refreshing. A life so meaningful and full of joy that it will astound you.

Most Christians assume they understand His offer. They think they've accepted it. But their lives often tell another story. I see believers all over the world weighed down with weariness and care, living as if Jesus said somewhere in Scripture, "I have come to work you to death. I have come to push you like a slave driver until you drop, to make you feel guilty, and drained, and condemned for never doing enough."

But you know as well as I do, Jesus never said that to anybody.

What He said was this: "I am the good shepherd. I have come that you may have life, and have it more abundantly. My purpose is to give life in all its fullness" (John 10:10-11, NKJV, NLT).

I will admit, my situation was extreme. The obsessive-compulsive, people-pleasing, performance-driven perfectionism that gripped me surpasses anything most Christians will ever experience. Yet most all believers fall prey to those things to some degree.

Women in particular tend to load up their lives with add-ons because they think their roles as wives and mothers demand it. They feel like it's their responsibility to make everybody happy all the time. Women tend to see it as their job to make other people's lives work, to help anyone who needs it anytime anywhere, regardless of the toll it takes on them.

Christian women, especially, have a hard time saying no. Whether the request is a serious one such as a sick friend asking for full time care, or a lightweight one like a football-watching family begging for nachos ("You cook, Mom, while we watch the game!") we find it hard to decline without feeling guilty. But here's a newsflash from heaven that applies to all of us: Jesus has set us free to say no. He has liberated us from the obligation to do everything people ask or expect of us and He wants us to exercise that freedom.

It's a simple truth but it absolutely saved my life. The day I realized—not just in my head but with my heart—that Jesus is a Shepherd, not a slave driver, the awful darkness and weariness that had plagued me began to lift. As I began to say no, with the help of the Holy Spirit, the guidance of the Word, and Ava's encouragement, burdensome add-ons that had weighed me down for years melted away like snowballs in summer. It was wonderful!

Except for one thing. After I got rid of the add-ons, I found there was very little left.

I'd always laughed when I remembered Jessica sitting in her car seat saying that she wanted her old life back. It was funny because at six years old, she didn't yet have much of a life.

It wasn't quite so funny for me to find out at 40 years old that I didn't have one either.

That Lovin' Feelin'

For weeks, Ava gave me assignments. "Go to a movie. In next week's session you can tell me whether you liked it or not," she said. "Read a book. Find out what you enjoy— fiction? biographies? Inspirational reading? What stirs your soul? Give me a report next time we meet."

Dutifully, I obeyed her. I figured there must be a personality buried somewhere beneath my habitual adapting and people-pleasing, and I was determined to uncover it. The process felt odd but interesting. It surprised me, really, to discover that the Lord didn't mind me enjoying myself. That He actually wants His children to have fun and that He will even join in.

Does it ever occur to you to go do something fun...and fellowship with God while you're doing it? It certainly had never occurred to me. I suppose it should have. After all, He did say that He would be with us always (Matthew 28:20). He did say that "I will never leave you nor forsake you" and that "God... gives us richly all things to enjoy" (Hebrews 12:5, 1 Timothy 6:17). But still, I was shocked to discover that He would go to a good movie with me or read a book. What a delightful surprise!

One day, however, Ava gave me an assignment that curbed my enthusiasm. "This week I want you to find a friend," she said.

"What?" I asked, my eyes wide with disbelief, as if she had asked me to find Bigfoot. "How am I supposed to do that? I know how to buy a movie ticket, no problem. I can go to Barnes and Noble and grab a book. But finding a friend is much harder. I don't even know where to start."

Unimpressed by my protest, Ava set her notebook on the little table beside her chair and stood up to let me know our session was over. "Easy or hard, that's your assignment," she said. "Next time we meet, I want you to tell me what you've done about finding a friend."

Driving home, I stewed over my situation. It was ridiculous. How could a person be in ministry for 25 years and have no friends? I had acquaintances, certainly. Dennis and I knew thousands of people. Not just people, but other Christians! We had long-time ministry connections with other preachers. But other than Dennis—whom I'd always considered my best friend—I had no one.

How could that have escaped my notice for so long? Didn't it occur to me that having no close personal friends is abnormal and unhealthy? And if so, why didn't I do something about it?

Back at the house, I slouched on the couch and hugged a throw pillow, pondering my predicament. I knew I couldn't just call somebody up and say, "Hey, you want to get together and be friends?" How nerdy would that be? I'd sound like a kindergartener.

No, the first thing to do was find an event, something fun to serve as a kind of bait. Then, with the bait on the hook, I could call somebody up and ask them go do this fun thing with me. Yes, that would be a good way to fish for a friend.

Tossing aside the throw pillow, I picked up the newspaper and rustled through the Entertainment section. At first glance its offerings weren't very promising. Black-bordered ads checkered the columns of newsprint announcing the usual oddball stuff. *All Shook Up! The closest thing to Elvis!...Orpheus in the Underworld: an operatic comedy... Underground Music Showcase Featuring: The FLOBOTS and SNAKE RATTLE.*

I sighed and wondered how the underworld could ever be funny—operatic or not. And what in the Sam Hill is a FLOBOT? Then, turning the page, I saw the ad in big bold print: *THE RIGHTEOUS BROTHERS in CONCERT.*

How appropriate! The Righteous Brothers. Does God have a sense of humor or what? Somewhere in the back of my brain, the music started. *You've lost that lovin' feelin'... whoa, whoa, whoa...* What a blast from the past! My love of the Righteous Brothers was one of the few things from my teenage years that's could be considered wholesome—if not exactly righteous in the Biblical sense—and most of my potential friends grew up listening to them.

Giddy, I ripped the ad from the paper. Then I began to make my mental list of people to contact. *Now, let me think. I could call…no, probably not her. Maybe I should call…no, that would definitely be a mistake. Oh, I've got it! I'll call Carolyn first. She might not be a big Righteous Brothers fan but at least she won't criticize me for wanting to go. So I'll start with her.*

I picked up the phone and dialed her home number. No answer. I called her cell. No answer. I called her office. Her assistant said, "She's not in the office today, may I take a message?"

"No. No message, thanks." I hung up the phone. *Well, I'll just call someone else then.* Forehead furrowed, I tapped my fingertips together as I scrolled through my mental rolodex of acquaintances…and came up with nada. Nobody. Zero additional possibilities.

Carolyn was the only person I could think of.

It's pathetic, I know. But that's the way it was.

The next day, I called Carolyn again. Home first. Then cell. Then the office. "I'm sorry, Carolyn isn't in today, may I take a message?"

"No, no message. Thanks."

The following day I repeated the drill. And the day after that. By the third day, I'd gotten so chummy with the assistant that when she told me Carolyn still wasn't in, I felt free to come unraveled. "Where on earth is she?" I cried. "This is

Vikki Burke. I've been calling for days. I can't get an answer. None of my messages have been returned. I don't know what else to do and I NEED TO TALK TO CAROLYN!"

For a split second there was silence on the other end of the phone. *Oops. I must have scared the poor girl.*

"Mrs. Burke, is there anything *I* can do to help you?" she said. "Uh…I'm not sure. Do you like the Righteous Brothers?"

"Excuse me? Did you say The Righteous Brothers?"

"Yes. There's a Righteous Brothers' concert coming up and I'm looking for someone to go with me." *Oh…my…word. I cannot believe I just said that. I don't even know this woman.*

"As a matter of fact, I love the Righteous Brothers! Count me in—when is the concert?"

Well, at least I would have something to tell Ava.

***

We didn't pay much for the seats. I liked them, though. Tucked under the low-hanging balcony at the back of Will Rogers Auditorium, wrapped in cozy semi-darkness, they provided a perfect view of not only the Brothers themselves but the entire audience of middle-aged rock n' rollers. What a sight! Aging engineers with pocket protectors linked arms with hippy wives (and I mean that in every sense of the word) wearing broom skirts and swayed to the oldies we grew up with. On the row behind us, a gaggle of sixty year-old women whooped and squealed like teenagers.

Laughing, I nudged Jessica, who had joined our party at the last minute to sub for Dennis who was out of town. She rolled her eyes in mock mortification but secretly she was having fun. So were my newfound friends—the assistant and her husband. They clapped and sang and swayed with everybody else; and when a particularly romantic tune pushed them over the edge, they jumped into the aisle to slow dance like a couple of high school kids.

I watched them in awe. I'd never danced in my life. Not for religious reasons but because my inhibitions ruled. How would it feel to be that free? *Someday*, I thought, *I'll know*.

A few days later when Dennis got home, I recounted every detail of the concert. He listened, caring but cautious. He was still adjusting to how chatty I'd become since I'd started the sessions with Ava and gotten my liberation mandate from the Lord. Now, with these latest developments, he hardly knew what to think. What do you do with a woman who goes from sitting sullen and silent in the bedroom chair to inviting strangers to rock n' roll concerts? Stretching out his hand, he gave the polecat a tentative pat.

A few days later, he surprised me with The Righteous Brothers Greatest Hits album. I still have it on my iPod. I didn't know it then, but he was going to make sure there were more concerts in my future.

I love my husband.

Back to School

The dreaded Marriage Seminar came and went with no deadly effects. It didn't kill me to do it and, as far as I know, nobody who attended died as a result. (I'm sure some people suffered, though, because even with the help of the Holy Spirit, my part of the presentation was pretty pitiful.) As the seminar disappeared behind me in life's rearview mirror, I made plans to stay away from podiums and platforms for a long, long time.

God, however, had different plans.

He was ready to help me take another step toward getting my life back. Now that I had cleared away the rubble and excavated a bit of my personality, He apparently thought I was ready. So He sent me to Bible School. Not as a student, but as a teacher.

Nobody was more surprised about it than I was. During our years of ministry, it had been suggested a number of times that I teach a class at Jerry Savelle's ministry training center. Dennis and I knew the Savelles well and had worked with them often over the years. Their Bible School was not far from our home. Dennis taught there on occasion and it made sense that I should do it too.

It made sense to everybody but me, that is. I thought the idea was awful. I liked working behind the scenes, being invisible. I've already told you how I felt about public speaking. So whenever the idea came up, I just smiled and thought, *No way am I going to do that.*

Having refused to teach even before the meltdown, I thought it doubly absurd when, right on the heels of my sessions with Ava (they ended because she moved out of town), I received yet another invitation. *If these people had a clue what a mess I've been for the past year, they'd be horrified,* I thought. *They wouldn't let me be a student, much less a teacher.*

All set to flex my thank-you-but-no-thank-you muscles, I was stunned when the Holy Spirit stopped me. *Say yes,* He said.

"Lord, You can't be serious."

Say, yes. I want you to do it.

"You're sure? You actually want me to teach a Bible School class?"

Yes.

"What am I going to teach about?"

Righteousness.

To be honest, I couldn't see that I had much choice. I had already made an agreement with the Lord: I would take the responsibilities He gave me, and He would give me rest, refreshing, and a life worth living. I knew He would keep His part of the deal. And though it never occurred to me that teaching a Bible School class would be involved, I meant to keep mine.

Shaking my head, I paused a moment to pity the poor students. I supposed that God would help them survive. "Okay, I'll do it," I said. I had no idea the invitation would forever change my life.

People tease me about being such a maniac about planning. Their teasing is justified. I can't deny it; I love to plan things. Obsessive-compulsive tendencies aside, I revel in organization and order. I especially love to plan out a journey. Every year, Dennis and I go on a road trip that takes us a couple of weeks and a few thousand miles. The trip is fun, yes, but planning it is more than that. It's ecstasy.

Mapping out routes. Finding good hotels. Accumulating brochures about points of interest along the way. Locating *you-just-gotta-eat-here!* restaurants. It all puts me into such a state of bliss that when I'm finished, I feel no need to take the trip. For real. Sometimes, after I've planned our vacation, I ask Dennis if we can cancel it because the best part is already over.

Some Christians are wary of people like me. They think planning isn't very spiritual, that it grieves the Holy Ghost. I know it's true because one minister actually said that to me. I felt ashamed of my love for planning for a while after that, but God eventually got me over it. (The shame, not the planning.) He reminded me that He planned out our salvation before the foundation of the world. I decided that put me in good company and I went back to planning again.

Because a good planner likes to start at the beginning, I prepared to teach the Bible School class on righteousness by opening my Bible to Genesis, the Book of Beginnings. It was a good decision. The only good one I made for the next two weeks. I hate to admit what threw me off course but I figure since it happened to me it could happen to you, so I'm going to tell on myself.

I went right back into perfectionist/people-pleasing mode.

The dean of the school, knowing I hadn't taught there before, showed me how he formatted his classes. He thought it might help me to know that he liked to spend the first 10 minutes of each 50 minute session reviewing the previous week's material, teach new material for 30 minutes, and use the last 10 minutes to review what he just taught. He didn't tell me I had to do it this way. He wasn't trying to force me into his mold. But I assumed his way was right, so I tied myself in knots for the next couple of weeks trying to adapt to it.

I poured myself into the task until I was ready to tear my hair out. Finally, I faced reality; I couldn't teach this class someone else's way. Risky as it seemed, I had to do it the way it worked for me. I had to stop trying to perform and meet other people's expectations and simply follow the leading of the Lord in my heart.

If you're anything like I was, you can understand what a major leap of faith it took to do that. When you've spent much of your life looking to others to guide and affirm you, it can be scary to break out of the mold they have cast for you. It takes boldness and faith to stand on your own and say, "I can hear from the Lord just as well as any other child of God. He is my Shepherd and I know His voice. Jesus promised, and I believe, that the Holy Spirit teaches me all things." But it's an essential step on the path to freedom. So I gathered my courage and took it.

There was just one hitch. By the time I did, the first class was only two weeks away—and those two weeks included the Christmas holidays.

Cloistering myself in the upstairs bedroom that doubled as an office, I sat at my desk surrounded by books, Bibles and computer. Across from me, bay windows let the winter sunshine drench the room with warmth and cheer despite the frigid temperatures outside. Downstairs, the Christmas tree, oblivious to my absence, twinkled merrily. Tiny white stars of light peeking through branches honored Jesus' upcoming birthday and blinked a silent warning that the Bible School classes would soon begin.

Praying fervently for help from on high, I opened my Bible to Genesis 1.

In the beginning God created the heavens and the earth. The earth was without form, and void; and darkness was on the face of the deep. And the Spirit of God was hovering over the face of the waters. Then God said, "Let there be light"; and there was light. And God saw the light, that it was good; and God divided the light from the darkness. God called the light Day, and the darkness He called Night. So the evening and the morning were the first day. Then God said, "Let there be a firmament in the midst of the waters, and let it divide the waters from the waters." ...Then God said, "Let the waters under the heavens be gathered together into one place, and let the dry land appear"; and it was so.... Then God said, "Let the earth bring forth grass, the herb that yields seed, and the fruit tree that yields fruit according to its kind, whose seed is in itself, on the earth"; and it was so... And God saw that it was good.

Genesis 1:1-6; 9; 11

The verses were so familiar I almost could have quoted them by heart. Yet I sensed that day something was different. Maybe it was because I was reading them in search of fresh revelation. But whatever the reason, it was as if I could hear something in the words that I'd never heard before. A kind of subtle drumbeat. Like a heart. The heartbeat of God.

I began reading again, listening for it more intently.

Then God said, "Let there be lights in the firmament of the heavens to divide the day from the night; and let them be for signs and seasons, and for days and years; "and let them be for lights in the firmament of the heavens to give light on the earth"; and it was so. Then God made two great lights: the greater light to rule the day, and the lesser light to rule the night. He made the stars also. God set them in the firmament of the heavens to give light on the earth, and to rule over the day and over the night, and to divide the light from the darkness. And God saw that it was good.

Genesis 1:14-18, NKJV

Trees. Lights in the firmament. Sun. Moon. Stars. My mind flashed to the Christmas tree showing off its splendor

85

to the empty room beneath my feet. What a pity it would be if no one ever saw it! What a waste if there was no family to gather around, no joyful eyes to reflect its sparkle, no eager hands to tear paper from the presents so tenderly wrapped! I thought of the hours of effort that just one simple Christmas tree required. What it took to buy it, drape it with lights, hang every ornament in the perfect spot. Yet all that was nothing compared to the power and planning required to create the universe.

I lifted my eyes from my Bible and looked through the arched panes atop the bay windows into the bottomless blue sky. In the afternoon light, I couldn't see the planets and stars and galaxies swimming out there in its oceanic expanse. Yet I knew they were there. How amazing to think they were all created by God with one purpose: To serve the earth. To mark its times and seasons. To give it light.

Somewhere at the back of my mind, questions nibbled at the thought. Why was the earth the reason for creation? Why was it so important to God? Why was He so particular about it?

No haphazard ball of dirt launched into orbit on a whim, the Bible says God weighed out earth's waters in the hollow of His hand. He measured the heavens with a span, calculated the dust of the earth in a measure, weighed the mountains in scales and the hills in a balance (Isaiah 40:12). God planned this planet with precision. He created it with breathtaking beauty and filled it with gifts of His goodness. But why?

The answer was obvious and simple. He wanted to provide a magnificent home for the family He had planned. He wanted to bless beyond measure the sons and daughters His heart had been yearning for.

My heart lurched under the weight of the revelation, tilting my internal world oddly off balance. This is how God set His family plan in motion. He said, "Let there be..." He spoke. Again and again. God said and kept on saying until everything was ready for the children that He wanted. And behind every word that He said echoed the heartbeat of love.

Cradling my Bible, I wrapped my heart around the realization: My Father framed this whole universe with words of love. And He did it...for me. The very ground of my being heaved and shifted at the thought. Two worlds collided within me—the old and the new.

The axis of the old had been set, not by God's words, but by the words of my parents. It had been set when in the innocence of childhood, I'd heard my mother say, "I never should have had children." Unwanted. Unloved. Born into a household completely unprepared for me. That had been my own personal creation story. I'd tried hard to bury it, but all my life it had been inscribed somewhere on the shores of my soul. I had never given the Holy Spirit the opportunity to rewrite it.

Until now.

The Bridge God Built

Not knowing whether to laugh or cry, I marveled at the difference between my earthly parents and my Heavenly Father. They had stumbled into a family on impulse and regretted it. He planned His family with foresight and love before time began. They had children and realized too late they didn't have sufficient resources to provide for them. He anticipated every need His children would ever have and provided for them in abundance ages in advance.

I had to chuckle. Compared to God, I was a rank-amateur in the world of planning. Come to think of it, compared to Him, I was like Dennis! Mr. Laid-back himself, Dennis waves away questions about the future with efficient grace, like a horse swishing away flies with its tail. (No hidden inference there, honest.) "What are we going to do about this thing that's coming up in a few months?" I'll ask him. "What's the plan for next year?"

"I haven't thought about it," he'll say. "We'll cross that bridge when we come to it."

My comeback—half joke, half rebuke—is this: "Dennis, I will have that bridge built, painted, lit and landscaped before you ever get there. I'll be the one who makes sure it's safe for you to cross!"

"Great!" he'll say. "See you there."

Sometimes Dennis's carefree ease frustrates me. But on that particular afternoon, the thought of it filled me with gratitude because I realized that God had actually done for me what I joked about doing for Dennis. He'd foreseen everything that would ever happen to me. He looked down the corridor of time eons ago and saw the jagged chasm of pain that would split the life of a little dark-haired girl in southern California. Long before I was ever born, He saw my need and planned to meet it. Long before sin marred the perfection of creation and separated not only me but all mankind from God's presence, He built the bridge that would span the breach.

He built it with His love. Painted it with His blood. Lit and landscaped it with the truth of His Word. And sent the Holy Spirit to get us safely across it.

A gust of wind rattled the windows of my cozy bedroom-office. Outside, the boney, bare-branched oaks huddled together in the backyard and shivered. *God has always been with me*, I thought, *even in the barren winters of my life.* He was there the day I lifted skinny arms to the sky and begged to die. Though I didn't know it at the time, the gentle wind of His love was already blowing over me, moving me toward this moment of revelation.

God, in His great love, denied my childhood death wish because He had already made other plans for me. Good plans, as the Bible says, plans to give me hope and a future.

Enveloped in the reality of God's love, I propped my elbows on the desk, rested my chin in my hands and steeped myself in the moment. The books that lined the shelves in the hutch above me stood guard like wise little soldiers. So many books about God. So many books brimming with Scriptural truth. Yet none of them had opened my eyes to this: that Jesus was there the day my dying father had failed, one last time, to tell me that he loved me.

My spirit leapt at the realization. Jesus saw the whole scene in advance. If the veil between heaven and earth had been lifted, I could have looked into His eyes and seen His love for me. I could have heard Him say, "Vikki, it's going to be okay. I'm going to take away this pain. I have a destiny for you and I've built a bridge that will get you there."

Picking up my Bible, I began to read again:

Then God said, "Let the waters abound with an abundance of living creatures, and let birds fly above the earth across the face of the firmament of the heavens." So God created great sea creatures and every living thing that moves, with which the waters abounded, according to their kind, and every winged bird according to its kind. And God saw that it was good. And God blessed them, saying, "Be fruitful and multiply, and fill the waters in the seas, and let birds multiply on the earth." So the evening and the morning were the fifth day. Then God said, "Let the earth bring forth the living creature according to its kind: cattle and creeping thing and beast of the earth, each according to its kind"; and it was so. And God made the beast of the earth according to its kind, cattle according to its kind, and everything that creeps on the earth according to its kind. And God saw that it was good.

Genesis 1:20-25, NKJV

I couldn't get over it. How many times had I read those verses without seeing the picture they paint? A picture of a loving Father supplying everything His family would ever need or desire. A picture of Love laying the foundation of a home. Love filling its skies with birds and butterflies, its gardens with flowers and foliage, its streams with sleek and shiny fish, its soil with silver, diamonds, platinum, and gold.

I laughed out loud at the part about diamonds and gold. God knew in advance what women would like. In my mind's eye I saw the time before my mother died, when Jessica was little and I took her to visit. Jessica had discovered Mom's jewelry box that day. Helping herself to everything in it, she put rings on every finger. She loaded her chubby little wrists with bracelets. She draped multiple strands of gold and pearls around her neck. Mother and I didn't scold her for it. We were delighted to see Jessica enjoying herself.

That's how God is! He loaded this earth with amazing abundance so that His children could have all they wanted and never run out. God filled this earth with limitless bounty because He was planning a family for whom He would have limitless love.

Then God said, "Let Us make man in Our image, according to Our likeness; let them have dominion over the fish of the sea, over the birds of the air, and over the cattle, over all the earth and over every creeping thing that creeps on the earth." So God created man in His own image; in the image of God He created him; male and female He created them. Then God blessed them, and God said to them, "Be fruitful and multiply; fill the earth and subdue it; have dominion over the fish of the sea, over the birds of the air, and over every living thing that moves on the earth." And God said, "See, I have given you every herb that yields seed which is on the face of all the earth, and every tree whose fruit yields seed; to you it shall be for food. "Also, to every beast of the earth, to every bird of the air, and to everything that creeps on the earth, in which there is life, I have given every green herb for food"; and it was so. Then God saw everything that He had made, and indeed it was very good.

Genesis 1:26-31

This is what it was all about. This was God's dream all along. He didn't dream of great corporations or governments. He didn't dream about economic structures or other things the world considers important.

God dreamed of a family.

That was His heart's one desire. It's what He longed for more than anything else. Children He could walk and talk with. Children He could teach to rule and reign by faith just like He does. Children who would share His heart and His nature, who would love and obey Him, not because they had to do it but because they wanted to.

On that chilly December day in Texas, the California beaches of my youth seemed worlds away. Yet in an instant, I was there again feeling the warmth of the west coast sunshine on shoulders, the damp grit of the sand beneath my bare feet, the warm waters of the rising tide tickling my toes. I remembered how, standing at the ocean's edge, the receding waves would pull sand from under my feet. How the very ground I stood on would slip away.

It was happening again now. But in the most wonderful way.

Somewhere on the beaches of my soul words had been carved decades ago. *Unwanted. Unloved. The child who should never have been born.* The devil had tried to harden those words into stone, to etch them on my consciousness forever. But he had failed. The revelation of God's love, like the incoming tide, was washing them away and leaving in their place a divine love letter written not only to me, but to you and anyone else willing to read it.

Dearest child, I created all this for you. Apart from you, there is no reason for it. No reason for beauty, no reason for the earth at all. You, dear one, are the fulfillment of My eternal dream. You are no accident, no mistake. I planned you before the world began. I saw you while you were yet unborn and longed to have an unending love relationship with you. I have always loved you and I always will. You can do nothing to earn that love and nothing to lose it. It is yours just because you exist...just because you are My child.

Forever,

Your Father

The Night God Played the Jukebox

Long ago, even before he made the world, God loved us and chose us in Christ to be holy and without fault in his eyes. His unchanging plan has always been to adopt us into his own family by bringing us to himself through Jesus Christ. And this gave him great pleasure.

Ephesians 1:4-5 NLT

If I've heard it once, I've heard it a hundred times. *God loves us not because of who we are but because of who He is. He loves us not because of ourselves but in spite of ourselves. Unlovely as we are, He loves us anyway because He is love.*

Such statements sound good in church. They seem religiously correct and appropriately humble. They even make sense, especially when we consider the condition we were in before we made Jesus the Lord of our lives. As Romans 3:23 says, back then we were all sinners who'd fallen short of the glory of God.

That's putting it nicely. To be more blunt about it, before God fished us out of the sewer of sin, we all stunk—through and through.

Most of us cleaned ourselves up after we got born again, thank heaven. By the grace of God we were able to change for the better. But even so, most of us couldn't quite shake the shame of that old sinful aroma. We wanted to smell like a spiritual rose, but we didn't. Sometimes in secret, we wondered how anyone as lovely as the Lord could even stand to be around us.

Maybe that's not every Christian's story. But it's the story of many believers. It may be yours. And most certainly, it was mine. For the first 25 years of my Christian life, I tried to rewrite it. I struggled to overcome my inward sense of unworthiness with outward accomplishments. But no matter how I perfumed my life with good works, deep inside I still felt unacceptable, inferior, and ashamed.

Mentally, I knew that God loved me, but somehow that knowledge failed to penetrate my heart. It failed to help me feel better about myself. The reason for my dilemma— complex as it seemed at the time—was simple: I was lacking a vital piece of the spiritual puzzle. Although I understood that God loved me, as He loves all of us, I didn't know why.

For years, believers have bought the religious lie that there is no *why*. That God's loving nature drives Him to love us irrationally, for no good reason. That His love says everything about Him but nothing about us. We are just the unworthy objects upon which He chooses to focus His affection.

That's bunk.

Let me ask you something. How would you respond if your husband or wife said, "Honey, I love you but there's no good reason for it. You're not worthy of my love. You're a totally unacceptable failure, a real stinker, but I can't help myself. I'm just so wonderful that I love you anyway."

Does that make you feel all warm and fuzzy inside?

No, it doesn't. That kind of love isn't satisfying at all.

Yet it's the kind of love we often attribute to God; the kind many of us learned about in church; a love that is not only unconditional, but irrational. Given how unlovable we feel, the idea that God's love for us is the result of a sort of benevolent insanity on His part makes sense to most of us. It especially made sense in my case. How else could I explain God's relentless pursuit of my soul? What possible sane or rational reason could He have had, to love a teenage girl who had broken almost every rule in His book and then decided to hate Him with all her might? A girl who had assessed the tragic little drama of her life and named Him as the ultimate villain.

Unanswered Prayers

Some people remember the first time they fell on their knees in church as the time they found God. I remember it as the time I rejected Him. I was 16 years old. My mother, panicked because my father was dying, had suddenly become religious.

Before then, she'd treated the Catholic church (to which she claimed to belong) like a piece of heirloom china to be used only on holidays, if at all. But as cancer dragged my dad closer to the grave, church became a weekly ritual, not only for my mother but for my younger brother and me as well. Neither of us wanted to go, of course. But she gave us no choice.

Herding us into the austere, unfamiliar chapel to attend mass, she ordered us to kneel in the aisle so that, while other congregants gawked at us from the pews, we could beg God to save our father's life. Angry and humiliated, I detested doing it. The flickering altar candles and the swish of priest's robes did nothing to soften the experience. Head bent in piety, hands folded beneath my chin, I seethed inside and prayed things my mother never intended. "If this is what I have to do for You to heal my dad," I said, hurling the words silently heavenward, "I hate You."

Later, alone in my bedroom, fear and remorse would set it. Hoping my earlier prayers had missed their target and fallen back to earth without causing harm, I prayed again. Tears leaked from the corners of my eyes and pooled on my pillow as I lay on my bed and cried out in earnest. "God, please, heal my dad. Please…"

Those prayers, too, missed their mark. My father died in spite of them. Furious, I pointed the finger of blame squarely toward heaven. In my young mind, my dad's death was God's fault. Hating Him was my revenge.

It wasn't just Him I hated, either. In my father's absence, the fullness of my hatred for my mother burst forth as well. For years, I had wished her dead. I say this not because it was justified but to reveal just how bitter my young and hardened heart had become. Many people consider parent-killers to be the most worthless specimens of humanity. Few feel any mercy for kids like the Menendez brothers who murdered their mother and father. Can even God find anything worth loving in such children?

Yes, He can. I know because I was a Menendez brother in the making.

As I saw it, my mother's death was the only thing that would free me and the rest of our family from her abuse. I wanted to kill her myself, but I never had the courage or opportunity to do it. There were times when my father, however, almost did. One day, walking up the sidewalk to our house after school with books bundled under my arm, I heard my mother's terror-stricken voice echoing inside the house. My step unhurried, I went to the door and put my hand on knob. It didn't turn. The door was locked.

Entering through the back door, I saw my mother lying on the floor begging for her life as my father held a gun to her head.

When my father looked up and saw my face, I locked eyes with him and communicated without words but with absolute clarity: *Do it*. Then I turned my back and walked away.

Much to my dismay, my father could never bring himself to pull the trigger. So my mother outlived him. After his funeral, I warned her that the tide had turned. "You've abused me for 16 years and I've taken it," I said. "But those days are over. It's payback time. I will torment you for the rest of my life."

My siblings shared my rage. From time to time, my sister and I even talked about things like putting LSD in Mother's coffee. We dreamed together about ending her tyranny over us once and for all. One day, after my mother screamed and struck out at me one time too many, I acted on those dreams. Hatred boiling over, I grabbed her by the throat. My fingers tightened around her neck. She struggled to pry them loose but my grip, like my heart, was unforgiving.

Blue-faced and suffocating, she began to wilt.

My mother survived my attack not because I relented, but because my brother jumped me from behind and pulled me off of her. She was grateful for his intervention. I was not. Wrenching free from his grasp, I responded to him with a single, dagger-like word: "Traitor!"

An Unlikely Evangelist

Can you see any good reason why God would want such a violent, hate-obsessed girl? Most people can't. Truth be told, most Christians—even those like you, perhaps, who were much nicer than I was even before you were saved—can't imagine what God sees in any of us. Think about it. Do you have any idea what it was about you that compelled God not only to die for you but to pursue you until you accepted His salvation?

I certainly didn't. Even after I was saved, it amazed me to think about how He came after me, how He tracked me down, not so that He could judge me and toss me into hell, but so that He could forgive me and draw me into relationship with Him.

It seemed ridiculous, really. But there's no denying that He did it.

I didn't realize it at the time, of course. It didn't once occur to me the day I sat on the beach at 19 years of age, watching my boyfriend surf, that a loving God was chasing me...and I was about to get caught. All I knew was that a yellow school bus had rattled to a stop in the parking lot on the cliff above the beach.

I might not have even noticed the bus if I hadn't sensed something powerful and unfamiliar in the atmosphere. It felt like a kind of unseen Presence was invading the place. I had no idea where it was coming from but I sensed it so clearly that even in the summer sun, I got goose bumps. Looking around for the source of the unexplainable Presence, I saw the bus in the distance high above me.

Young people streamed out of it, dressed not in swimsuits but in street clothes, and onto the steps leading down to the beach. It was obvious they were geeks, alien to California. No self-respecting west coast-er would come to the ocean dressed like a junior higher on the first day of school. Whatever these kids were up to, I wanted nothing to do with them or the freaky Presence that preceded them. So I stretched out face-down on the sand as if I was sunbathing and pretended to be asleep.

My possum act, however, failed to protect me. As the rest of the group filtered down the beach, two of the teens—a boy and a girl—drifted my way. To my horror, they stopped and settled themselves in the sand beside me. Then they did something even worse. They started talking to me about God.

Clean cut kids from Michigan on a church sponsored mission trip eager to witness to beach bums and hippies, they may or may not have been prepared for the response I gave them. It was swift and angry.

"I hate God!" I said.

If they were shocked, they didn't show it. The girl simply asked me why.

"Because He killed my dad," I answered.

I can't remember now what they said in response. I only remember that with the rhythm of the surf in the background and the gulls squealing overhead, they kept on talking. Telling me about God. About Jesus. About divine love.

Red-faced with anger, I gritted my teeth and reaffirmed to them my hatred of all things divine. But even in my fury, my tears betrayed me. Unable to stop myself, I wept because somewhere inside I longed to believe that what they said was true.

When at last they stood up and, brushing the sand from their ridiculous clothes, indicated they were about to go in search of another lost soul, the girl who had introduced herself to me as Sherry Griffith, asked me one final question. "Would you mind if I sent you a Bible?"

"Yeah, that would be okay," I said. Hoping to rid myself of them as fast as possible, I jotted my name and address on the piece of paper Sherry handed me. *There,* I thought as I watched them clomp down the beach leaving shoe prints behind them, *that's the end of that.*

Little did I know, it was only the beginning.

A few weeks later, the Bible arrived. A paperback New Testament entitled *Good News for Modern Man*, it didn't look like I expected. (Then again, since I hadn't seen very many Bibles back then I really didn't know what to expect.) Fanning through the pages, I saw simplistic line drawings and scriptures highlighted in red and yellow. No doubt, Sherry had highlighted them because she thought they were especially important.

I didn't read them, however. I didn't read any of the *Good News for Modern Man*. The very idea terrified me. I'd been told by the priest during my rare visits to church that reading the Bible would drive a person crazy. A little on the crazy side already, I figured I shouldn't risk being driven further in that direction. So, pitching the Book in my dresser drawer, I tried to forget about it.

For some reason, however, I couldn't. A peculiar inner hunger kept drawing me back. Not daring to read the words, I skipped through the pages to find the pictures. Unlike the fancy full-color illustrations in traditional Bibles, these looked like doodles done by children. Sitting cross-legged on my bed, I poured over stick figures, circles, and crosses that summed up the plan of salvation. They were fascinating, for sure. But they seemed to be a kind of spiritual hieroglyphics that for the life of me I couldn't decipher.

What I needed was translator.

So God sent me one.

It's easy to slip into generalities when we talk about how much God loves us. After we're saved and sitting scrubbed-clean in church, we often forget how God donned His waders and sloshed around in the sewer to find us. We soften the hard-edged reality of His quest by saying simply that God will go to the ends of the earth to reach a lost soul. Such statements are true, of course, but they don't capture the startling picture of how passionate and personal this God who is so in love with humanity—so in love with you and me—can be. They don't remind us of just how intimately He knew us and how humbly He pursued us even when we were running from Him.

That's why I like to remember who God chose to translate for me the mystery of the Gospel. He didn't pick a preacher. (I didn't trust preachers.) He didn't pick a goody-two-shoes from the local youth group. (I would never have listened.) He didn't pick a Sunday School teacher.

He picked Gary. My ex-boyfriend. The love of my life since the seventh grade. The drugged-out guy I'd dated and dreamed of marrying but didn't because even in my messed-up condition, I knew that he would bring me nothing but trouble. The guy who had infuriated me and broken my heart a few months earlier by calling to tell me he was leaving for Seattle and disappearing from my life.

Two thousand years ago, Jesus came to the world in a manger that smelled of half-eaten hay and cow spit. In 1971, He came to me through a long-haired hippie who, just months before, had smelled of marijuana and Jack Daniels. I don't know a religious person on earth who would have picked Gary to be an evangelist back then.

But God apparently wasn't interested in being religious. He was interested in getting the attention of a teenage girl.

First the Devil, Now God!

I got Gary's letter on December 30, my birthday. Heart thumping, I ripped open the envelope and read his short note: *Just want you to know that I miss my girl. I've started reading the Bible....I'll see you soon. Gary.*

Somehow the part about reading the Bible escaped my notice. All I saw was that Gary was coming home, and I was planning to give him a very warm welcome (if you get my drift). A few weeks later, he called and I jumped behind the wheel of my Volkswagen Beetle and beelined toward his house.

The second he opened the door, I knew he was different. He had the same face, the same body, but he was not the same person. Inside his house, I saw no alcohol bottles, no cigarettes, and no baggies stuffed with illegal substances. This was definitely not the Gary I'd previously known.

Sitting me down in his room, he placed a Bible between us and told me that he'd given his life to the Lord. I had no idea what that meant. Then he said that Jesus was coming back soon. I had no idea what that meant either. Then he said, "Vikki, after the earthquake hit Los Angeles a few weeks ago, God spoke to me. He told me to come back here and tell all my friends about Jesus."

Once again, I had no idea what he meant but I went rigid with fear when he said God had spoken to him. It was the second time since the earthquake in February (the worst quake on record at the time) that somebody had told me a "spirit" had spoken to them. The first time had been a couple of weeks earlier when a girlfriend and I had picked up a pair of hitchhikers on our way to the lake. After an afternoon of skinny dipping, we'd shoplifted some steaks for dinner and come back to her apartment to smoke some joints.

Between tokes, one of the hitchhikers told me about a recent, hair-raising encounter he'd had with a woman who claimed to be the devil. He said she communicated with him telepathically at a party and when he doubted her claim, she proved it. As I listened, wide-eyed with terror in the haze of her smoke-filled apartment, he described how he'd seen another being—a supernatural entity—emerge from the woman's body. "It was the devil!" he said. "I swear it was. He came out of her, then went back in. I saw it with my own eyes."

Laugh if you will, but the story scared the liver out of me. So when Gary said that God had spoken to him, I panicked. *First the devil, now God!* I thought. *What on earth is going on?*

Oblivious to my reaction, Gary kept talking. He told me things he'd learned from studying the Bible with his friend, a born-again Christian in Seattle. He asked me to read some scriptures with him but I deferred for fear of going crazy.

Laughing off my reluctance, he read them aloud to me. Scared but excited, I hung on every word.

When he read me the parable of the ten virgins, I could hardly contain my amazement. "I can understand that!" I said.

Gary assumed I meant that I'd grasped the significance of the parable, but that's not what I was saying. I had no clue what the parable actually meant. What thrilled me was hearing the Bible in English. Until then, I'd only heard it recited in Latin by a priest. So when I said I understood, I meant it in the most basic way.

Captivated by the Bible readings and everything else Gary had to say, I listened, transfixed, for hours. The next day, I called in sick and skipped work so that I could go back to Gary's and learn more. On the third day, I called in sick again. For three days straight, I listened to Gary talk about Jesus. Then he told me he was going back to Seattle.

When he invited me to come with him and meet the Christian friends he'd gotten to know there, I jumped at the chance. Calling my employer, I begged for some time off, packed my bag and headed north.

During the next few weeks, I leapt with eager curiosity into Bible studies, church services, and impromptu chats with radical young members of The Jesus Movement. Much of what I heard was over my head but I tried my best to keep up. I did okay until the night the group invited me to go with them to The Catacombs. All I knew about catacombs was what I'd seen in movies about early Christians carving fish symbols on cave walls and being fed to lions. I recalled with a shudder that martyrdom, blood, and bone-crunching were involved. I didn't know if I was brave enough to give up my life for Jesus, but if my new friends were willing, I was determined to try.

That evening, I huddled together with other believers, sipped coffee in The Catacombs and awaited my demise. How I could have been so worldly and yet so naive at the same time I can't say; but I truly expected lions to lunge from the shadows at any moment. As guitar-strumming musicians crooned worship tunes, I marveled at how calm my friends seemed to be, but I couldn't match their courage.

Somewhere around midnight, I slipped out of The Catacombs into the darkened, deserted streets of downtown Seattle and ran for my life.

Ashamed of my cowardice and wondering if I could ever be a true Christian—*would Jesus even want a lily liver like me?*—I ducked into an all-night diner. The place was quiet as a cathedral. Every booth was empty, every Formica table-top bare. A solitary waitress stood at the cash register sorting through receipts while I sat, slumped in a booth, nursing a glass of ice-water. (I didn't have money for anything else.)

Then, all by itself, the jukebox began to play a song I'd never heard before.

"Amazing Grace" by Judy Collins.

Looking back on that moment now, I'm astounded to think about what happened to me in the years afterward. How in my first few decades as a Christian, I began to feel so unworthy to come into God's presence. How He seemed to me to be a thousand miles away, keeping His distance, arms crossed, face somber, and eyebrow arched. How I began to see Him as unapproachable and myself as unacceptable.

Where could I have gotten such an impression? Why do so many Christians have it? How could we ever think such things about a God so forgiving and so kind?

This is a God of infinite gentleness and compassion. This is a God who created the universe in all its splendor with us in mind. This is a God who sent His Son to die on our behalf. This is a God who can fall so in love with a mixed-up, messed-up, teenage girl that He will follow her into a diner at midnight and play a song for her on the jukebox.

Just to win her heart.

And win it, He did.

As the words of "Amazing Grace" washed over me for the first time, I was changed forever. My heart and my life were never again my own. From that moment on, I belonged to Jesus—the Savior and Lover of my soul.

I understood very little back then about where my relationship with Him would lead me. All I knew was this:

I once was lost but now I'm found, was blind but now I see.

Answering the Question

Most of us start out in life asking *why*. If you doubt it, spend some time with a four year-old. Kids that age want to know the *why* behind everything. They can wear out a parent in an afternoon asking why birds sing, why the sky is blue, why mosquito bites itch, why Daddy has to go to work, and why they can't eat chocolate cake for supper.

At one time or another, most parents run out of patience, opt for the easy way out, and give the answer we've all heard. "Just because."

When that happens, kids usually stop asking why.

The same thing happens to Christians. When we're first born again, we're eager and inquisitive. We ask questions and search for answers. If we can't find them in the Bible on our own, we ask our spiritual elders. Sometimes, we get the answer we need. Other times, we hear the curiosity quenching phrase, "Just because."

That's the answer most believers get when they ask why God loves us. We're told He loves us *just because*. Just because He's God. Just because He's love. Just because, for some arbitrary reason, He decided to do so.

Unsatisfactory as such answers are, they would be okay if the issue was unimportant. If God's love was simply a matter of religious trivia—like whether or not white shoes should be worn on Easter in southern churches where white is deemed unfashionable until after Memorial Day—we could accept any old explanation of it. But there's nothing trivial about knowing why God loves us. It's something we absolutely must understand. It's something that can make or break our relationship with Him.

Sad to say, I didn't realize that the night I heard "Amazing Grace" in the diner. If I had, the first 25 years of my Christian life would have been very different. Instead of packing them with performance and frenzied efforts to win God's approval, I could have spent them enjoying His fellowship. I could have walked and talked with Him, learning with confidence and freedom the lessons He was eager to teach me. I could have relaxed knowing that, while giving correction when necessary, He was watching my spiritual growth with pleasure. He was continually rejoicing over me, clapping His hands and saying, "Vikki, you're *good!*"

"Oh, I could never imagine God saying such a thing about me," you might say.

This may come as a shock, but He already did.

He said it about all of us.

You know when I found that out? In the days before Christmas as I was preparing to teach the Bible School class on righteousness. After I'd been a Christian for a quarter of a century.

It wasn't until after I'd almost killed myself trying to prove my worth that I realized God had already established it. He even had it written down in the first chapter of Genesis so that I could read it. (I guess He thought that surely I would read at least the first chapter of His Book.) There, the Bible says that the day God created mankind, He looked at everything He had made—including us—and said "...indeed it was very good" (Genesis 1:31 NKJV).

"But that was before Adam and Eve sinned," you might say. "That was before the fall of man."

I know. We'll talk more about that later. But for now, it's enough to say this: Mankind fell and Jesus fixed it. He took care of the sin problem so that what was written in Genesis 1:13 can still be said about every born-again believer today. *Indeed, we are very good.*

Actually, to say we're good is an understatement. The Scriptural truth is, we're God-like. We're created to be as close to deity as we can possibly be. God made us living, breathing, copies of Himself. He said:

"Let Us make man in Our image, according to Our likeness; let them have dominion over the fish of the sea, over the birds of the air, and over the cattle, over

all the earth and over every creeping thing that creeps on the earth." So God created man in His own image; in the image of God He created him; male and female He created them.

Genesis 1:26-27

Man-made religion can't handle these verses. It downgrades them to mean that God made human beings *a little* like Himself, that He created us *kinda, sorta, vaguely similar* to God but also vastly inferior to Him. That might sound right to us. It might seem humble. But it's not what this passage says.

It says that God made man in His *likeness*. Strong's Exhaustive Concordance defines likeness as "an exact duplication in kind." In other words, God created us in His class of being. He reproduced Himself in us so that He could have true fellowship with us. He didn't make us to be like the animals. He didn't want pets; He wanted children. He wanted a family.

I don't care what PETA says, pets aren't the same as family members. Dogs are not man's best friend. There's a massive, qualitative difference between people and animals. Certainly animals can learn some things. They can be fun to have around. I used to have a dog named Maggie who knew according to what shoes I was wearing when I was leaving the house. When I put on the outside shoes, she'd run to the door and twirl in circles jumping and barking because she wanted to go with me. She even figured out that when we said goodbye we were going somewhere. (She got confused about it, though, after we subscribed to an Internet service that said goodbye when we logged off.)

Maggie knew some fun stuff but I couldn't really have much fellowship with her. If I took her somewhere in the car, she couldn't sing along to the Oldies with me when I played them on the radio. She couldn't have a conversation with me. She couldn't talk with me about life because she's not like me. She was created in a different class. She's not a duplication of my kind of being.

When I want true fellowship, I don't look to Maggie. I look to Dennis or Jessica or one of my friends.

When God wants true fellowship, He looks to us.

I know that's a staggering thought but it's true. God made us for the purpose of fellowshipping with Him. He created us like Himself so that we could respond in kind to His love, so that we could commune with Him on His level. He duplicated Himself in us in every way except in this: we are dependent on Him, and He is not dependent on anyone or anything.

This is not just a theological concept, it's reality: We are God's children. And just as human children are born looking like their parents and not like a dog or a monkey, God's children are born looking like Him spiritually. That's why the New Testament admonishes us to "… be imitators of God as dear children" (Ephesians 5:1 NKJV). We can imitate Him because we are made according to His *likeness*!

If that's not stunning enough, Genesis 1:26 also says we're made in His *image*. Again, according to Strong's Exhaustive Concordance, an image is "a representative figure." That means we were created as exact duplications of God so that we could represent Him on earth.

Psalm 115:16 says, "The heaven, even the heavens, are the Lord's; But the earth He has given to the children of men." It was God's joy to give mankind dominion over the works He created. It pleased Him to give us, as His sons and daughters, the privilege, power, and responsibility to rule this world.

According to the Bible, all of heaven witnessed man's creation. Think how much it must have startled the angels to see God going to the Garden of Eden to visit man every day. They must have said the same thing that the author of Psalm 8:4-6 said:

What is man that You are mindful of him, And the son of man that You visit him? For You have made him a little lower than the angels, And You have crowned him with glory and honor. You have made him to have dominion over the works of Your hands; You have put all things under his feet...

Although in our English translations, verse 5 says that God made man a little lower than the angels, the Hebrew word rendered "angels" is actually *Elohim*. In other scriptures, it's translated "God." Genesis 1:1 says, "In the beginning, God [*Elohim*] created the heaven and earth." Bible translators, thinking of man in his fallen state, couldn't believe that God created us just a little lower than Himself, so they chose to use the word "angels."

The Bible, however, is clear. God established our status as just under His own. Mankind became God's under-ruler. Humanity was given authority over all creation. The very elements of the earth and even the angels had to obey when they spoke, just as they obeyed the voice of God himself.

Can you imagine how beautiful and wonderful Adam and Eve were in the beginning? According to Psalm 8, they were crowned with glory and honor. The Hebrew word translated "crowned" actually means "encompassed." Adam and Eve were encompassed, surrounded, and clothed with the radiance and splendor of God's own glory.

Why does all this matter? Why is it important to you and me?

Because it answers the question, "Why does God love us?" It helps us understand why God considers us so precious, so worthy of His compassion. It lets us know that although God's love for us is unconditional, it is not irrational.

Let this sink in, my friend. Think about it until it saturates your heart. God doesn't love us in spite of ourselves. He loves us because He knows who we were truly created to be. He loves us because He can look beyond the temporary affects of sin and see us through His plan of redemption, restored to our original condition, crowned with glory and honor, exact duplicates of Himself with whom He can walk and talk and fellowship on His own level.

Even before we were born again, God saw in us the children He always dreamed of. He saw in us the most magnificent, God-like beings ever created; men and women so divine that on the day God made them, all of heaven caught its breath in awe.

"But what about our sins?"

Washed away by the blood of Jesus.

"What about all our flaws and imperfections?"

God looks past them the way a loving parent might look past the dirt on a mud-caked child. No matter how much we cover ourselves with the soil of this temporal world, He sees beneath it the sons and daughters who look so much like Him, the beautiful children He holds so dear.

"Long ago, even before he made the world, God loved us and chose us in Christ to be holy and without fault in his eyes" (Ephesians 1:4). And so we are.

That's why He loves us so much. That's why He chases us through the mud puddles and sewers of sin until He can catch us and wash us clean. That's why He follows us onto beaches and into diners. That's why He hunts us down and sings to every one of us, in one way or another, the message of His amazing grace.

CHAPTER **6**

The One Thing

"But one thing is needed, and Mary has chosen that good part, which will not be taken away from her."

Luke 10:42

If *Jeopardy* had a category called Dumb Choices Made by People in the Bible, this would surely be one of the answers: *She chose to go in the kitchen and make tacos when Jesus was teaching, live and in person in her living room.*

The question: *Who is Martha?*

Granted, the Scriptures don't actually say anything about tacos. That comes from my own paraphrase of the story. I've always imagined, because of my Mexican heritage, that Martha's meal preparations on that infamous day involved tortillas, lettuce, and cheese. What else do you serve a house full of unexpected guests?

The Biblical account of the story, however, goes like this:

Now it happened as they went that He [Jesus] entered a certain village; and a certain woman named Martha welcomed Him into her house. And she had a sister called Mary, who also sat at Jesus' feet and heard His word. But Martha was distracted with much serving, and she approached Him and said, "Lord, do You not care that my sister has left me to serve alone? Therefore tell her to help me." And Jesus answered and said to her, "Martha, Martha, you are worried and troubled about many things. But one thing is needed, and Mary has chosen that good part, which will not be taken away from her."

Luke 10:38-42 NKJV

In the 2,000 years that have passed since Martha's ill-conceived dinner, literally thousands of sermons have been preached about it. Untold numbers of Christians have marveled over her muddle-headedness. Tsk-tsking about her mistake, we've wondered how she ever made it. I mean, really, who in their right mind would go in the kitchen to chop onions when the Creator of the Universe is sharing His wisdom in the living room? Wouldn't any sound-minded believer be like Martha's sister, Mary, and stay as close to Him as possible?

No, we wouldn't; and every one of us has proved it. At some time in our lives, we've all been Marthas.

Some Christians like me actually surpass Martha. We get so busy, so "worried and troubled about many things" that we not only neglect to sit at Jesus' feet for an afternoon, we do it for years on end. Trading fellowship with the Master for frenetic service, we turn into Martha-on-steroids.

For years, I was the poster child for that kind of Christianity.

But here's the thing; I didn't start out that way. I started out more Mary-like. In my first few months as a believer, I spent almost all my free time alone in my apartment reading my Bible. I didn't even go to church in the beginning. My Jesus Movement friends had warned me when I left Seattle that God didn't attend any of the churches in Los Angeles so I should stay away from them. I promised I would do so, and for a while it was just Jesus and me. At home. Alone.

Ultimately, though, I got lonely. I wanted to talk to and hang out with other Christians. The problem was, I didn't know anybody. All my old friends were still up-to-their-eyeballs in sin and totally uninterested in getting out. Other than going to church, I had no idea how to connect.

One Saturday morning in July, unable to stand the solitude another second, I closed my Bible, hung my head, and apologized to the Lord. "I'm sorry to be such a wimp," I said, "but I've got to have a friend. Will you please send me one? I don't care what kind of friend it is—fat, skinny, old, young, male, or female—as long as it's someone who knows You."

A few hours later, puttering down the street in my Bug on my way to check out a new apartment, I spotted the answer to my prayer. *Jeff Eggars!* He was standing on a corner, hugging what looked to be a dictionary (unabridged, no doubt, because it was massive) under one arm, engaged in animated conversation. I pulled the car to the curb and jumped out to get a closer look. Yep, it was Jeff all right.

His appearance had changed dramatically since I'd last seen him. Head wreathed in hair from crown to chin, he looked like a mountain man or a monstrous Chia Pet. But beneath his fuzzy pelt he was still the same Jeff that I'd known in school.

I was unfamiliar back then with the leading of the Holy Spirit so I didn't understand why I felt drawn to Jeff that day. Last time I'd seen him he wasn't a Christian. Neither was his girlfriend, whom I'd particularly despised back in our high school days and harassed without mercy.

How I suddenly knew that the dictionary under Jeff's arm was actually a gargantuan Bible, I couldn't explain. But I was certain of it; just as I was certain that Jeff had become a Jesus Freak like me. I figured that I could confirm it if I could get close enough to hear what he was saying to the person he had buttonholed on the street.

I sighed and hesitated. Maybe Jeff wouldn't remember my fights with his girlfriend.

Angling myself his way, I strolled across the sun-baked concrete as if I was heading to the store down the block. When I got within earshot, I heard Jeff say something about Jesus. The rumble of traffic drowned out the last part of his sentence but I'd heard enough to be certain of this: he was witnessing.

Stepping up next to Jeff, I broke into the conversation. "You can believe what this man is saying to you," I said, motioning toward him. "He is telling you the truth."

Jeff turned and stared at me open-mouthed, as if a passing pigeon had fluttered in to say a few words. It was obvious he didn't recognize me. My looks had changed as much as his. Even if he had seen a resemblance to the Vikki he used to know, he would have discounted it upon hearing my enthusiastic endorsement of the Gospel.

I hurried to re-introduce myself and a flurry of hugs and exclamations followed. Jeff was thrilled to hear about my newfound faith and, after sharing with me about his own relationship with the Lord, he asked me if I'd found a church yet. "No," I said. "God isn't in Los Angeles so it's dangerous to attend church here."

Jeff guffawed. "Who told you that?"

He shook his head as I repeated what my friends from Seattle had said. Then he launched into a description of the church he attended and the group of young people there who were totally sold out to Jesus. "We're actually having a meeting at the church tonight," he said. "Would you like to come?"

When I climbed back into the Bug and headed toward home, I glanced heavenward through the windshield. It seemed I owed God yet another apology. "I'm sorry, Lord, if it's a sin to go to church here. If it is, I guess You'll just have to forgive me because I'm going to the service tonight."

That church turned out to be my new home; the covey of young people, my new family; one of them became my husband.

Work or Worship?

There is nothing wrong with being busy for Jesus, nothing inherently Martha-ish in it. It's a delightful experience to be about the Father's business doing the "good works, which God prepared beforehand that we should walk in them" (Ephesians 2:10). The Lord wants us to be eager to do those works (Titus 2:14), and during my first few years as a believer, I was eager as can be. So was Dennis.

We both showed up at church for almost every activity. We volunteered for anything they would let us do. We did visitation. We went witnessing. We attended Sunday services, Wednesday services, Bible studies, and fellowship meetings. After a while, I even went to work for the church. I was there seven days a week!

Back then, I wasn't working to prove myself. I wasn't trying to gain anybody's approval. I was just head-over-heels in love with Jesus and overjoyed to be saved. Sad to say, that didn't win me any brownie points with the elders at church. In fact, it aggravated them. They counseled Dennis and me to tone down our exuberance. They tried to tamp down our spiritual fire because we were making them look bad.

They issued grave warnings such as, "If you're too heavenly minded, you'll be no earthly good." That pearl of wisdom mystified me. It still does. Being heavenly minded is a good thing. This earth needs as much of heaven as it can get.

I shrugged off the fact that the elders weren't as excited about what God had done for them as Dennis and I were about what He'd done for us. I didn't know what their problem was but I couldn't help myself. I'd been delivered from hell—not just the afterlife kind of hell but a hellish life here on earth. How could I be anything but excited about it? Oblivious to everybody else's opinion, I threw myself with childlike abandon into serving the Lord.

I'll admit it: I was busy making tacos even back then. But it was okay because I was making them with Jesus. I was chopping onions while sitting at His feet.

Those were good days. But they didn't last.

Somewhere along the way, I went to the kitchen.

I lost sight of the Master and began to work for the wrong reasons. My service began to be driven by duty instead of delight, by the need to prove my worth and please people, by my desperate desire to earn God's approval and overcome my sense of guilt, shame, and inadequacy. That's when I became a Martha. That's when I stopped enjoying my life in Jesus and started getting irritable just like she did.

One reason I identify with Martha is that in the beginning, she had good intentions. She invited Jesus to her house because she wanted to be a blessing. She was led by God to open up her home to Jesus and His entourage, which included at least 70 people. Her motive was right; she wanted to give Him a place to teach.

If she'd stuck with her initial leading, Martha could have had an awesome day. When the crowd got hungry, she could have handed Jesus a bowl of beans and asked Him to multiply them. She could have said, "Lord, I'm determined not to miss a word You have to say. I want to spend time with You more than anything else in the world. So, if You want these people to eat, You can feed them. If not, we'll all just fast until You're finished teaching. Either way, I'm not leaving Your side."

But Martha didn't say those things. She added to her original leading and decided she had to turn the event into a dinner party. She took on the pressure of it—self-induced pressure—and went into performance mode. Then she did what we all do in that situation. She got mad.

Standing in the kitchen, pounding out the tortillas, she starting fuming about Mary sitting in there on her backside enjoying herself. *That lazy sister of mine*, she thought, *she always does this, leaves me to cook, leaves me with all the responsibility. If I don't do everything, nothing gets done.*

Finally, she couldn't stand it anymore. She marched into the living room where Jesus was teaching and interrupted Him. "Lord, doesn't it seem unfair to you that my sister just sits here while I do all the work?" she said. "Tell her to come and help me" (v. 40).

Isn't that always the way we do? When we get irritated, stressed, overwhelmed, and under pressure, we get resentful and bitter. We blame everybody else. Martha not only blamed Mary for her situation, she faulted Jesus too. She as much as said to Him, "Don't you care about me? How can You sit there and teach while I'm doing all this work?"

(Here's something to remember: It's always a mistake to blame God when things go wrong. He's never the problem, He's always the solution.)

Instead of defending Himself or shooing Mary into the kitchen to help her sister, Jesus did something else altogether. He put an end to the blame game. He let Martha know that she was not a victim. Jesus pointed out that both she and Mary had been given the opportunity to spend time with Him.

Martha had chosen to pass up that opportunity and work instead. She devoted herself to doing.

Mary had chosen to worship. She devoted herself to being with Jesus. Mary was hungrier to hear the voice of the Lord than she was for tacos. She desired His wisdom. She wanted, more than anything else, to receive all that God had for her.

Human doings vs. human beings. Doing the Master's work vs. spending time with Him in fellowship and in the Word. Which is most important? Jesus settled the issue. He said Mary made the best choice. She got her priorities right and put first things first.

In my own life, I learned the hard way that when we slip from Mary-dom to Martha-dom, we totally miss God's direction for our lives. We stop hearing His voice and run into all kinds of trouble we could have avoided. When we get too busy to take time every day to sit at Jesus' feet, when we let our lives get so hectic that we don't spend time daily reading His Word and just being with Him, we get off track. It's inevitable.

Oh, we may not run wild and get involved in gross, obvious sin. We may not rob the corner grocery store or cheat on our spouse or start sipping beer at the local bar. We may continue to go to church every Sunday and do so many good works that we look like model Christians. But the evidence of our Martha-dom will be there nonetheless. We'll get irritable and feel sorry for ourselves. We'll start pointing the finger of blame at others (including God) and resenting them for not doing more to help us.

We'll find ourselves running on empty, trying to fix everybody's life, trying to be the savior in all kinds of situations, and winding up exhausted. That's what happens when healthy, happy Christian service turns into perfectionism and performance. And it's not pretty.

A Universal Problem

One thing I discovered after I became a human doing, melted down, and ended up in Ava's office was that my story isn't unique. Martha and I aren't the only ones who started out with good intentions and then veered off course by leaving our place at Jesus' feet. It's a common pattern among believers.

Shockingly common.

I found that out in my first few weeks of counseling while reading a book Ava had given me. I felt so ashamed about what I was going through back then that I sighed with relief to find the book full of stories about people just like me. "Listen to this, Dennis!" I would say, more eager to blurt out my latest discovery than he probably was to hear it. "Here's a story about someone named Helen (or Sarah, or Michael) who ran into the same problems I did!"

I regaled Dennis with one such account after another in those days. (Bless his heart.) One in particular that stood out to me was about a young man named Jeff. His story only filled a few paragraphs of the book but it seemed especially important because it was so ordinary, so normal. I like to share his story because not everybody can identify with the trauma that marked my childhood. Most believers, however, can relate to Jeff.

He grew up in an ordinary way, as a typical kid. His relationship with his parents had a few glitches (whose doesn't?) but they were nothing catastrophic. Mostly, he just struggled to win his parents' approval, and he often felt that he failed. As years passed, a sense of insecurity and inferiority began to dog him both at home and at school. (Is there anybody who *didn't* feel insecure in junior high school?)

Then, in his early 20s, Jeff became a Christian. Initially he was ecstatic. He felt he'd finally found the love and acceptance he always wanted—both through his relationship with the Lord and his friendship with other believers.

After a while, however, Jeff's joy began to fade. He didn't feel as loved anymore. He began to suffer the same old pangs of insecurity and inferiority. Assuming it was somehow his fault, he slipped back into old, familiar patterns. As a kid, he'd coped with such feelings by working hard to earn the approval of his parents and peers. So he did the same thing when he began to feel he wasn't quite as accepted and loved by the Lord.

He tried to do whatever he could to please Him. That solution led him only to empty perfectionism before; now it led him to strict legalism. There seemed to be plenty of people at church who knew lots of things Jeff ought to do to please God, so he tried to do them all. He

124

attended every meeting, read the Bible religiously, and gave away lots of money, but instead of feeling closer to God, he felt that God was increasingly distant, harsh and demanding. His want-to freshness in those first months of his relationship with the Lord had become a stifling, condemning, have-to burden. Though he did a lot for God, he seemed to feel more and more distant from God.[4]

Apparently, even men can have the Martha syndrome.

In fact, it is practically universal.

"But Vikki," you might ask, "if that's true then why don't we hear more about it at church?"

Because most church leaders don't recognize it. Even if they did, they might be reluctant to mention it because they depend on Martha-types to keep the church programs going. It's the truth. Most Christian organizations value Marthas more than Marys. Why shouldn't they? Marthas are always helping, fixing, volunteering, working ridiculous hours, and doing whatever the pastor says needs to be done. Marthas make great church workers because they are efficient and seemingly tireless.

Martha-dom is generally applauded and rewarded as evidence of a deep commitment to Christ. On the outside, that's what it looks like. But the inner workings of it are all wrong. Unlike the Mary kind of serving which is a response to the unconditional love and acceptance of God, Martha service is driven by fear (lack of faith in God's ability to handle things), guilt, and a need to achieve worth.

Marys are led by the Holy Spirit.

[4] Pat Springle, *A Christian Perspective / Codependency Emerging from the Eclipse*, Edited by Susan Joiner. (Houston, TX: Rapha Publishing, 1989) p. 104.

Marthas are driven by the devil's lies.

Months after I finished the book Ava had given me, I began to see exactly what those devilish lies are. I realized that they're rooted not in our own, personal psychology, or the particular mistakes our parents made, but in what happened more than 6,000 years ago in the Garden of Eden. It became startlingly clear to me as I studied for the Bible School classes on righteousness: Performance-driven Christianity is not a new phenomenon. It wasn't unique in Martha's day and it's not unique in ours. It started in the very beginning with a slimy serpent and a woman named Eve.

Sitting in my little bedroom/study with my Bible open to Genesis, I read the first few chapters again and again as the truth began to dawn on me. I thought about how in the early days of their relationship with the Lord, Adam and Eve were like many new Christians are right after they are born again. They centered their whole lives around fellowship with God.

Talk about a couple of Mary-types! Adam and Eve depended on the Lord for everything. They weren't idlers. They had work to do. God had given them the responsibility of tending the Garden and guarding it against intruders. But they were never too busy for the Lord. They walked with Him and talked with Him every day. They fellowshipped with Him in the cool of the evening.

They knew that God loved them—not for what they did but for who they were. And in His presence they enjoyed life to the fullest.

Then the devil showed up.

Now the serpent was more cunning than any beast of the field which the LORD God had made. And he said to the woman, "Has God indeed said, 'You shall not eat of every tree of the garden'?" And the woman said to the serpent, "We may eat the fruit of the trees of the garden; "but of the fruit of the tree which is in the midst of the garden, God has said, 'You shall not eat it, nor shall you touch it, lest you die.'" Then the serpent said to the woman, "You will not surely die. "For God knows that in the day you eat of it your eyes will be opened, and you will be like God, knowing good and evil."

Genesis 3:1-5, NKJV

Here's the thing about the devil both in Adam and Eve's day and in ours; he never comes waltzing in wearing a red leotard, sporting horns, and waving a pitchfork. He's too crafty and subtle for that. He's the most skillful deceiver that ever lived. And his method of operation never changes. He always poses as a friend.

How do I know he posed as Eve's friend?

Because she didn't show any surprise when he started conversing with her. She didn't get suspicious when he referred to what God had said in a private conversation with her and her husband. This indicates to me that Eve and the serpent had talked about those things before. Maybe in a prior conversation, the serpent had sidled up to her, remarked about the beauty of the Garden, and chatted with Eve about it for a while. Maybe in the course of their visit she mentioned what God had said to them about the trees.

In my opinion, the Genesis 3 conversation couldn't possibly have been the first between Eve and the serpent because I don't believe she would have fallen for his trick that quickly. Surely it would have taken more than one question from a total stranger to get her to betray and disobey God. After all, she and Adam had a trusted, love relationship with Him. They knew Him.

Somehow the devil must have gained her confidence. He must have hung around and been friendly until she was convinced he posed no threat. He'd probably said some things that were true to put her off her guard. (He always mixes truth with his deception. We wouldn't fall for it otherwise.)

Three Devil Inspired Doubts

Obviously, Eve didn't know she was talking to the devil, the author of all evil. She didn't know she was chatting it up with an enemy who wanted to destroy her. But then, neither do we. When the devil slips into our thoughts and starts questioning God's goodness or distorting His Word, it rarely occurs to us to ask where those thoughts are coming from.

That was definitely true in Eve's case. Assuming the serpent was friend not foe, she took his musings and his simple query, *Hath God said...?* at face value. She never suspected there was danger in them. She didn't dream that wrapped inside the serpent's suggestions were razor sharp doubts. Doubts that, once entertained, would wound her heart and slash at her sense of worth. Doubts so terrible that they would deceive her into severing her relationship with God and result in the spiritual death of the entire human race.

When we read in the Bible about how it all happened, we usually focus on the end result of those doubts. We emphasize the fact that Adam and Eve ate the forbidden fruit, that they disobeyed God, and sinned. We stress the point that back then, as now, the wages of sin is death.

But as I studied the story on the heels of my own personal breakdown, what grabbed my attention were the devilish insinuations that preceded the sin. I saw as never before how the devil suggested that God's love couldn't be trusted, that He didn't really have Adam and Eve's best interest at heart; how he inferred that they were inferior and less than divine, that they had not been created in God's image after all; how he implied that they could improve their situation by depending less on God and more on their own knowledge and ability.

In short, the strategy the devil used against Adam and Eve was the same one he uses against Christians today:

- Make them doubt God's perfect, unconditional love.

- Make them doubt that they are truly like God, created in His image.

- Make them doubt that their relationship with Him is enough to make them significant, wise, and worthy.

That's more than just Biblical history. It's more than a three-point summary of how the devil destroyed Eve's relationship with God and, ultimately, her life. It's a description of what he's done to multitudes of good, God-loving people. It's what he did to Martha, to Jeff, to me, and to you.

Those three devil-inspired doubts are what have driven all of us, at one time or another, out of the peaceful place of fellowship with Jesus. They're at the root of all the add-ons in our lives, all the frantic efforts to win approval—God's and everybody else's.

When we start being driven by those doubts, life gets really hard. Ask the Pharisees about it; they know. By the time Jesus came on the scene, they'd added on 2,000 rules to what God had told them to do in the Bible. They put so many requirements on people that nobody could keep them all.

Sound familiar?

Of course it does. It's still happening today. We have requirements bombarding us from all sides. The world says we have to meet a certain standard of beauty, talent, wealth, education, and influence to be acceptable. We're constantly told what we should wear and how much we should weigh. Athletes and movie stars are paraded in front of us as examples of what we should be, and reminders of how far short we fall.

Those same attitudes have even crept into the church to a degree. People with a lot of money sometimes get front row seats and special meetings with the pastors. Church members who wear clothes from Nordstrom's and live in gated communities are treated as more significant than those who shop at thrift stores and live in efficiency apartments.

It's no wonder that so many Christians end up trying to earn their acceptance from God. It's simply proof that the devil is still at work. He is still selling the spiritual merit system. And believers are buying into it, even though the New Testament tells us over and over that we are unconditionally:

- "accepted in the Beloved" (Ephesians 1:6)

- "made the righteousness of God in him" (1 Corinthians 5:21)

- "children of God... born, not of blood, nor of the will of the flesh, nor of the will of man, but of God" (John 1:12-13)

- "the elect of God, holy and beloved" (Colossians 3:12)

- "saved through faith, and that not of yourselves; it is the gift of God, not of works, lest anyone should boast" (Ephesians 2:8-9)

The Ben Campbell Johnson paraphrase sums it up this way: "...Where unconditional love prevails, merit ceases to exist" (Romans 11:6).

Why then are so many of us still striving to be worthy of God's love? How did we end up sweating it out in the kitchen with Martha instead of enjoying ourselves at Jesus' feet?

Speaking for myself, I made the same mistake that she did. I got my priorities mixed up. I got so addicted to getting things done that I ran out of time for the Master. I fell for the devil's lies because I got too busy to hear the voice of the Lord.

Everything Else Can Wait

When Dennis and I take our once-a-year-just-for-fun road trip, we like to leave early in the morning before the sun comes up. I always want to be the first to drive. It doesn't matter to me if we head out at 3:00 a.m., I'm happy to do it because I'm a morning person. My eyelids tend to go down with the sun.

Every year it's the same. We throw the suitcases in the car before dawn; I slide behind the wheel; Dennis dozes; and I tune the radio into the Oldies station. I'm convinced the 1970s gave birth to the best music ever made, so I love to crank up the volume and bop my way down the highway. Somewhere around Abilene, however, a horrible thing happens: Country music cuts in. The Beatles give way to the sound of static and the Oak Ridge Boys, and my morning is wrecked. (Not that country music isn't wonderful. I'm sure it is. Just not to me.)

For a while, I put up with it. Fiddling with the buttons on the radio, I try to tune in Paul McCartney and tune out Willie Nelson. But the farther west I drive, the more Willie I hear. As far as I know, Abilene doesn't have an Oldies station so once the original is out of range, I turn off the radio and just listen to the wind. (There's never a shortage of wind in west Texas.)

It's a familiar experience and it's no mystery to me. I understand completely that when it comes to radio signals, the further you are from the source the more static you hear. Get far enough away and you'll pick up another signal entirely on what would appear to be the very same station. If I was more committed to the Oldies than to our vacation, I could make a U-turn, go back to Ft. Worth and enjoy more '70s tunes. I know that because I'm smart about radio station stuff.

Too bad that in the first few decades of my Christian life, I was not as smart about spiritual stuff. It didn't dawn on me that to stay tuned in clearly to the direction of the Lord, I had to stay close to the Source by fellowshipping with Him in prayer and the Word every day. I never considered the possibility that by straying from those times of fellowship, I might get my signals confused and wind up bopping down the road to the wrong tune.

But that's what happened. Somewhere in the first decade or two of my Christian life, I got too busy to do the one thing that is needful: spend time with Jesus. I kept telling myself, I'll do it later...or tomorrow. Days passed, then months, and years as I kept thinking, *One of these days I'm going be able to set aside some time to be with the Lord. One of these days, when things settle down at the office, when I finish some of the projects I'm working on at home, when I get this list of things done, I'll make prayer and the Word a regular part of my day.*

After 25 years of Martha-dom and a head-on collision with the 18-wheeler of burnout, this is what I figured out: If we don't put our time with the Lord first place in our lives, we won't get around to it. Other things will always steal it and we'll eventually become easy marks for the devil.

If that's never happened to you, you're blessed. But if it has, I want you to know that no matter what your personality type, no matter how busy your schedule, you can turn things around. I did—and when you consider the performance-driven, workaholic, approval addict I used to be, I think you'll agree that if I can do it, anybody can.

My secret?

Something I dubbed *planned neglect*.

Call it crazy if you want, but it works. Since I'm such a planner, I turned it to my advantage and started planning to leave the bed unmade, the dishes in the sink, or the laundry undone when necessary to make time to be with the Lord. If guilt tried to sneak up on me and the devil accused me of being a slacker, I'd just say, "No, I'm leaving those things undone on purpose. I have decided to make my prayer and Word time first priority. I will not allow anything else to pre-empt it. I am planning to let everything else wait."

If you have trouble with perfectionism, if you have workaholic tendencies that draw you away from your time with the Lord, get a piece of paper and write this down: *Everything and everyone else can wait.*

For me, that one phrase turned out to be the key to getting alone with God. It helped me focus on Him without my mind being pulled back to all the things I had to do. In the past 20-plus years as I've spent daily time with the Lord, I've proven it to be true. The business of the day can wait.

The kids can wait. The telephone calls can wait. They waited for me and they will wait for you. Once you've put first things first and spent some time at Jesus' feet, hearing His voice, getting built up, getting direction, reconnecting with His wonderful, unconditional love, everything else will still be there waiting.

It's an amazing thing.

I like to think that Martha eventually figured it out. I like to imagine that after Jesus told her that Mary had made the right choice, Martha straightened out her priorities. That she smiled, flopped down on the living room floor and said, "Teach on, Master. The tacos can wait."

CHAPTER 7

No Need to Hide

For you were once darkness, but now you are light in the Lord.

Ephesians 5:8

You've never heard of it unless you were a student in my class on righteousness, but I can guarantee that you've experienced it. It's been around since Adam and Eve. And every human being on earth has suffered from it at one time or another.

I call it *The Elliot Syndrome.*

Others, more eloquent and scholarly than me, refer to it by more sophisticated names. Like *sin-consciousness*, for example. Or *spiritual shame.* Those terms are excellent, to be sure. But I like mine because it brings to mind a dog I once owned named Elliot who—like those who share his syndrome—spent much of his life hiding.

Unlike human beings, Elliot didn't hide for deep, spiritual reasons. He simply detested going outside. The very idea of setting foot (or paw) beyond the threshold of our home into the great outdoors terrified him. I don't know why, but he had a phobia of being in the open where anybody and everybody could gawk at him. So he avoided it with vigor.

Whenever I put a leash on him, he wiggled out of my hands and tore around the house seeking refuge. Usually

135

he chose to conceal himself beneath a bed. Cowering under box springs and behind bed skirts, he seemed convinced I wouldn't find him.

But I always did. Quite easily, in fact. Because no matter how far under the bed he hid, his leash trailed out behind him and gave him away.

Poor Elliot. He wasn't exactly the brightest candle in the window. But, as I realized a few years later (after I'd handed him off to an owner more sympathetic with his habits), we can all identify with him. In one way or another, we've all tried to hide.

Personally, I started hiding young and stayed with it for years. I didn't actually see it as hiding, of course. The way I saw it, I was just shy. I liked to stay in the background. But the truth is, just like Elliot, I was afraid. Afraid somebody would notice me and ask about my life. Afraid that someday the whole sordid truth about my past—about myself—would come out where everybody could see it. Afraid, even after I was born again, that somebody would ask me the questions so common among believers. Questions like: *How did you get saved? Did you grow up in a Christian home? What first drew you to the Lord?*

It was bound to happen eventually. I'd always known it. Maybe my candle burned a little brighter than Elliot's, because I realized from the beginning that my leash was sticking out from under the bed and one day somebody would grab it and drag me into the open. I just didn't expect it to happen in front of 20 well-known, widely respected ministers. Ministers who'd be looking me in the eye for the next five days. At close range. From the other side of a raft.

It was the summer of 1987. I'd been saved more than a decade. Dennis and I, along with a bunch of sunscreen-slathered fellow ministers, had set out from Lees Ferry, Utah, on a rafting trip down the Colorado River. The day we launched, I was as excited about the trip as everybody else. Bundled in life jackets, with the spray in our faces and smiles a mile wide, we were headed for a week of adventure—riding the sun-kissed currents of the Colorado in the daytime and camping under the stars on the riverbank at night.

This will be great! I thought.

And, for a while, I was right. The first day, at least, was fabulous.

We finished it waterlogged and weary, but happy as clams. Our empty rafts dripping on the beach, we grappled with tent poles and canvas while the crew clanked pots and pans in a makeshift kitchen. The evening air cooled and thickened with the aroma of grilled steaks and coffee. A pile of driftwood, backlit by the last rosy rays of sunset, sparked, sputtered, and began to burn.

After dinner, all 20 of us stretched and yawned in front of the campfire. If we'd been teenagers, we most likely would have been overtaken by the need to sing "Kum-ba-ya." (It was truly a classic "Kum-ba-ya" moment.) But, maturity having gotten hold of us, one of the group piped up with another suggestion. "Why don't we spend some time each evening sharing with each other how we got saved?"

Everyone else chirruped their approval. I sat mute as a mackerel with what I hoped was a pleasant look plastered on my face. On the inside I screamed *No-o-o-o!*

This group of people had no idea where I'd come from or how I'd grown up. Although I'd known some of them for years, I'd never breathed a word about my past to a single one except Dennis. I felt certain many of them suspected the truth. No matter how I tried to hide it, I figured they could see through my church face to who I *really* was. But suspecting was one thing. Hearing the horrific facts confirmed out loud was another.

No longer happy as I clam, I suddenly felt just plain clammy. The night seemed colder. The campfire lost its effect. These people would reject me if they knew where I'd come from and what I had done. I was sure of it.

Panicked and hoping for a way of escape, I did the math. Twenty ministers, six nights. Even if two or three people shared each evening, we wouldn't get around to everyone. A few would finish this trip with their stories still untold.

Oh, Lord, please let me be one of the few.

Sometimes God takes a while to answer a prayer. This time He didn't waste a moment. He instantly let me know that I would be among those called on to share.

Mercifully, He didn't leave me in torment for days wondering when my turn would come. Dennis and I were selected the second night. When we stood up to share, I slid behind Dennis so he would have to go first. His testimony was ridiculously short and sweet: Raised in a happy family, went to church all my life, saved at nine, and here I am now in the ministry. It sounded like an episode of *Happy Days*. Thank you, Richie Cunningham.

When Dennis sat down, I cringed as the group stared at me expectantly. Crickets chirped. A frog ribbeted. Somewhere in the darkness, beyond the circle of firelight, the river shushed and splashed. I stared at my feet and searched desperately for something to say. There was nothing left to do but give a short version of the truth.

Condensing the story and omitting the details, I told about the abuse I grew up with, about the beatings, and the guns held to my head. I told about the hitchhiker who talked to the devil and the former boyfriend who preached to me night after night. I told about the jukebox and Judy Collins singing "Amazing Grace."

I'd run from this moment all my life. I'd dreaded it even as a kid. Waiting for the bus to take me to school, I'd refused to answer when the neighborhood children asked me why my mother screamed so often and so loudly. As a teenager, I'd protected myself from my friends' prying eyes by refusing to let them into my house. I literally locked them out so they couldn't see the filth inside.

If that didn't work, I'd simply lie, like I did late one night when a drunken teenage friend pushed past my front door and went into our darkened kitchen to get a drink. As she switched on the light, the walls crawled with cockroaches. She almost fainted.

"What on earth are those?" she shrieked.

"I don't know what you're talking about," I said.

"Those creatures all over the wall!"

"There's nothing on the wall. You're so drunk, you're hallucinating." Putting my arm around her in apparent concern over her condition, I guided her back out the door.

I'd lived my whole life hiding like that—and now here I was standing center stage in front of a bunch of preachers to whom I'd just divulged my secrets.

Elliot, in his worst nightmares, had never faced something like this. It was the worst case scenario. At least, it should have been. But the night God dragged me out of hiding,

139

something unexpected happened. People's expressions softened. Tears brimmed in the eyes of some and cascaded down the faces of others. Even the most rugged member of the group—a hulking fellow casting a shadow the size of a bear's—sniffed and swiped at his eyes with calloused hands.

Their tears gave me hope. Instead of rejecting me, they were being touched by what I said. Scanning the faces, I saw acceptance and compassion everywhere I looked.

As we all headed to our tents for the night, one person after another pulled me aside to thank me for sharing. The big minister with the tough hands and the tender heart added a special request. "Would you come and talk to the women in my church? Many of them have been abused. It would really bless them to hear you."

I nodded and gulped. As I struggled to swallow the beach ball that had inexplicably inflated inside my throat, someone behind me touched me gently on the shoulder. Turning, I found myself looking into the sweet face of one of the pastor's wives. "Vikki," she said, shaking her head in wonder, "I never would have known you'd gone through so much. I always thought you were a pure Christian girl who grew up in church."

The words rocked my world. My mind reeled as I tried to make sense of them. *Pure? She thought I was pure? How could that be?* I stared at her in silence, esophageal beach ball still fully inflated.

I could hardly believe it. This precious lady knew my history yet it was clear that she didn't see my horrible past. She saw me in the light of the work Jesus had done in my life.

Unaware of the quake she had triggered, she squeezed my hand. Then she said goodnight. I watched her disappeared into the moonlit darkness toward her tent feeling in my heart—perhaps for the first time ever—that I was indeed a beautiful new creation. That Jesus had washed away my shame. That I no longer needed to hide.

It would be a long time before I walked in the fullness of the revelation, but that night I took my first baby step. I began to see that maybe—just maybe—I could leave the Elliot Syndrome behind.

Eventually, I did. But it turned out to be a whole lot harder than I expected.

Victims of Identity Theft

It wasn't God who made it hard, of course. It was me. I mucked up the process by going back to my same old habits. At the end of that monumental seven day trip, as soon as we jumped out of the rafts onto shore of Lake Mead and headed for home, I went back into performance mode. I got busy, busy, busy.

It hadn't dawned on me back then that being busy was one of the ways I stayed hidden. If I'd been a Mary in those days and spent more time with Jesus, He would have revealed it to me. He would have shown me—long before I finally saw it in Ava's office—how I used perfectionism to cover up my sense of unworthiness. How I hid my sense of inadequacy behind my continual drive to overachieve. How I pushed myself to do...and do...and do...all the while secretly hoping that by doing I could become the person I so desperately wanted to be.

If I'd given Him the opportunity, the Lord would have taught me way back in 1987 the revolutionary truth I learned years later: *That* do *is only half of* done. *So when we're not living in the reality of what Jesus has already done for us, no matter how much we do, it is never enough.*

Oh, how true I proved that to be! The more I did to work my way out of my unworthiness, the deeper into the performance pit I fell. The more I did to overcome my inadequacy, the more inadequate I felt. Nothing I achieved on the outside could change the fact that on the inside I saw myself as a fallen, inferior creature. Even though I was born again, I still felt like "just an old sinner saved by grace." Even though I'd been given a brand new spiritually identity, I still suffered from the same poisoned mindset that plagued Adam and Eve after they disobeyed God in the Garden.

Sad to say, I put up with that mindset for ten years after the rafting trip was over.

When did it begin to change?

By now, you know the answer. It changed as I studied for my Bible School class on righteousness. As I dug into the Book of Genesis I saw my own story reflected in Adam and Eve's. I saw that when it comes to suffering identity crises— like the one I'd been stuck in for so long—they take the prize.

They were, without a doubt, the first true victims of identity theft.

In the beginning, they knew exactly who they were: the most spectacular creatures in the universe. Children of God created in the perfect image of their Father, they were as pure as God is pure. They were righteous with His own righteousness. They had no sense of inferiority or inadequacy. Untouched by shame, guilt, or fear, they walked in confidence with God himself. They talked with Him face to face. They strode the earth as a king and queen, divinely appointed and anointed rulers, crowned and robed with the blazing light of God's own glory.

Most Christians don't realize just how magnificent Adam and Eve originally were. They picture them running around in the Garden bare as a couple of babies in a bathtub and too naive to know it. But that's not how it was. Eden wasn't the first nudist colony. Adam and Eve were clothed from the inside out. Covered with a garment of glorious light, they looked just like God as the prophet Ezekiel saw Him—as a fire from the loins up and a fire the loins down (Ezekiel 1:27).

That's why they were, as the Bible says, naked but not ashamed. Their physical bodies could not be seen through the brightness of the glory that surrounded them. They looked absolutely dazzling.

When Adam and Eve sinned, however, all that changed in an instant. Dethroned by the devil, they lost their very identity.

Their sin disconnected them from the life of God. The light of His glory that once radiated from within them went dark. Suddenly, they saw their own nakedness.

Even worse, they felt an awful inward change. The devil had lied to them and told them if they ate of the tree of the knowledge of good and evil, they would be like God. But just the opposite happened. They became *unlike* Him instead. By yielding to Satan's temptation, Adam and Eve had made him their lord and their spiritual father (John 8:44). As a result, the divine nature within them became perverted. They were born again from spiritual life to spiritual death, from light to darkness.

Can you imagine the awful, unfamiliar feelings that must have flooded them at that moment? Just think how ashamed they felt! How guilty and defective and unrighteous! All at once, Adam felt less than a man, less than the son of God he was created to be. Eve felt less than a regal daughter of the Almighty. For the first time in their lives, the once-royal couple felt insignificant, lonely, and afraid. Their beauty had turned to ashes; their purity had been corrupted.

Where once they had been conscious only of their righteousness, now they were conscious only of their sin.

What did they do about it?

They hid—from each other and from God.

> ... they sewed fig leaves together, and made themselves aprons. And they heard the voice of the LORD God walking in the garden in the cool of the day: and Adam and his wife hid themselves from the presence of the LORD God amongst the trees of the garden. And the LORD God called unto Adam, and said unto him, Where art thou? And he said, I heard thy voice in the garden, and I was afraid, because I was naked; and I hid myself.
>
> Genesis 3:7-10 KJV

What a tragedy!

In former days, Adam and Eve had run to meet God when He came to visit. They probably called to one another like eager children, "Hurry, let's go see the Lord. I hear Him walking in the Garden. I can't wait to find out what He's going to teach us today!" But after they sinned, they cowered in the bushes. They shivered with shame and worried about how angry and disappointed with them God would be.

It's absurd, I know, but it seems that Adam and Eve actually thought they could hide from God. They seriously entertained the idea that He might not be able to find them.

Didn't they know they were like Elliot with his leash sticking out from under the bed? Did they really believe they could conceal their fallen condition with a few fig leaves and a little shrubbery? Do we?

Whatever they might have been thinking, God knew what Adam and Eve had done long before they told Him. He's omnipresent and omniscient. He knows and sees everything. He understood full well the terrible treason they'd committed.

And here's what's amazing about Him—He sought them out anyway. He went to find them when they were at their very worst. He called out for them because, even in their fallen condition, He still loved them. Nothing they could do would change that. No sin they committed would make Him reject them.

His love for them, like His love for us, was unstoppable.

If they'd only understood that love and trusted it, Adam and Eve could have run to God instead of hiding from Him. They could have confessed their sin and asked for help and forgiveness. That's what God wanted them to do. It's what He wants us all to do. But they didn't do it because they were more conscious of their guilt than they were of God's forgiveness. They were more conscious of their fallen condition than they were of God's ability to lift them out of it. They were more conscious of their sin than they were of God's commitment to deliver them from it.

So they covered themselves up. They tried to make themselves acceptable again by doing something. They got busy making fig leaf suits. It didn't work, though. They soon discovered, as we all do, that in the presence of the Lord, even the finest fig leaf suit leaves you feeling underdressed.

Solving the Identity Crisis

Speaking for myself, I spent years feeling like Adam and Eve did the day they lost their glory clothes and ran for the bushes. I lived much of my Christian life feeling woefully, embarrassingly *underdressed*. Like I'd shown up for the prom in my pajamas.

I don't mind admitting it because every person on the planet has felt that way. Unbelievers feel it because as descendents of Adam and Eve, they carry within them the imprint—however jaded—of the divine. They know somehow that they were created to be glorious and regal. It's woven into their DNA. So, try as they may, they can't escape the nagging sense that they are far less than they were meant to be.

In the case of unbelievers, this is perfectly logical. They feel underdressed for life and for fellowship with God... because they are. They feel sinful because they're sinners. They are afflicted with feelings of faultiness and inadequacy because they've not yet accepted the cure for that affliction—the saving, cleansing power of Jesus' blood.

No surprising news there. What's surprising (or should be) is this: The majority of Christians feel the same way. Even though they're born again, even though they've made Jesus Christ the Lord of their lives, they still feel ashamed inside. They still feel flawed and unacceptable. They feel like failures, like they are a disappointment to God.

No wonder they don't run to their prayer closet to spend time with Him every morning. No wonder they rush off to string together more fig leaves. No wonder they're so busy doing...and doing...and doing. They haven't gotten the revelation that through Jesus, what they're trying to do has already been done! They're still seeing themselves, like I did for so long, as just an old sinner saved by grace.

"But Vikki, isn't that what we are?"

No, it's not. The Bible says:

> *... if anyone is in Christ, he is a new creation; old things have passed away; behold, all things have become new. Now all things are of God, who has reconciled us to Himself through Jesus Christ...For He made Him who knew no sin to be sin for us, that we might become the righteousness of God in Him.*
>   2 Corinthians 5:17,18,21, NKJV

As believers, we're no longer members of a fallen race. Through the new birth we've become a new species of being. God "has created us anew in Christ Jesus" (Ephesians 2:10). The divine identity, the purity, the dominion, the godlikeness that Satan stole from Adam and Eve in the Garden has been restored to us on the inside. Our spirit has been reunited with the Lord. We've been made righteous again!

Righteousness is absolutely vital. It's what gives us confidence in the presence of God. It puts us back in the condition Adam and Eve were in before the fall. Because we've been made righteous, we can run to God with the wide-eyed eagerness of children. We can come with confidence into His presence without any sense of guilt, sin, condemnation, or shame.

We don't have to hide anymore!

Why then are so many Christians still under the bed?

Because they haven't renewed their minds to their new identity. They haven't fully grasped the reality that, through Christ, they've been made a new creation.

147

They still think of themselves as the same old sinner they used to be—saved and forgiven, yes, but embarrassingly flawed. They see themselves like spiritual criminals who've been freed from prison by a governor's pardon. They're thankful for the pardon. They're grateful that Jesus paid the price for it so that they can go to heaven instead of hell. But in their minds, that doesn't change who they are. They are still just sinners pardoned by grace.

The real message of the Gospel, however, is much more powerful than that. It declares that we've not only been pardoned, we've been reborn. We've become:

- "a new person, created in God's likeness—righteous, holy, and true" (Ephesians 4:24)

- "partakers of the divine nature" (2 Peter 1:4)

- "children of God...righteous, just as He is righteous" (1 John 3:1,7)

- "conformed to the image of His Son, that He might be the firstborn among many brethren" (Romans 8:29)

- "holy and without blame before Him in love" (Ephesians 1:3)

- "blameless and harmless, the sons of God, without rebuke, in the midst of a crooked and perverse nation, among whom ye shine as lights in the world" (Philippians 2:15)

It doesn't matter how wicked a person is, once he makes Jesus his Lord, he's like a newborn baby. He has no history of sin. His spirit is perfectly pure and righteous. Where once he was darkness, now he is light in the Lord (Ephesians 5:8) because...

*...the righteousness of God which is by faith of Jesus
Christ [is] unto all and upon all them that believe: ...
For all have sinned, and come short of the glory of God;
being justified freely by his grace through the redemption that is in Christ Jesus:*

Romans 3:22-23

To be *justified* means to be declared free from guilt or
blame, to be expunged, cleared, and pardoned of all wrong
doing, just-as-if we'd never sinned.

If that's not enough to convince you it's safe to come out
of hiding, here's another thrilling bit of information. Your
justification wasn't just part of a package deal that you were
lucky enough to get in on. You're not just one of a million
beneficiaries of a kind of spiritual class action suit. No, the
Bible says that you were *chosen* by God (Ephesians 1:4). Talk
about special! Talk about significant! You were handpicked
by the Creator to be His own child.

The apostle Paul used the term *adoption* to describe what
God has done for us. He said that God...

*...predestined us to adoption as sons by Jesus Christ
to Himself, according to the good pleasure of His will,
to the praise of the glory of His grace, by which He
has made us accepted in the Beloved. In Him we have
redemption through His blood, the forgiveness of sins,
according to the riches of His grace which He made to
abound toward us...*

Ephesians 1:5-8 NKJV

Isn't that awesome? We're actually God's children twice-
over. We're born of Him and adopted by Him.

Whenever I think of adoption, I remember how a friend
of mine and her husband chose each of the five children

they adopted. It was such a precious process. They studied the children's pictures. They read all the information about them. They prayed over those children and then picked the ones best suited for them. My friends fell in love with those children before they ever met them.

The same is true of us. God fell in love with us before we were born. As God's adopted children, we should never feel rejected. We should feel selected. Accepted. Chosen. Tenderly picked and dearly loved. New creations made righteous with God's own righteousness. Reborn in the very image and likeness of God.

Because that's what we are.

Complete the Journey

I hope all you dog lovers will forgive me for this but as I already mentioned, I eventually got fed up with Elliot. I tired of chasing him around the house multiple times a day. I wearied of trudging from room to room in search of the telltale leash and dragging him, toenails dug into the carpet, out from under the bed. So I got rid of him. I gave him away.

In my estimation, he wasn't worth all the trouble. He was, after all, just a dog. (I have another, much more cooperative one now.)

People, however, are different. We *are* worth the trouble. God certainly thinks so. He's proven it time and again.

He proved it in the Garden when He called out for His fallen children and said, "Where are you?" He proved it right on the heels of their rebellion when He sacrificed an animal for them and covered their nakedness with tunics made from its skin. He proved it when He sent Jesus to the cross to redeem His lost sons and daughters. And He keeps proving it every moment of every day by seeking us out wherever we may be hiding, by parting the shrubbery, peering under beds, and saying, "There you are!"

But even as committed as He is, God can't do everything for us. We, too, must do our part. We must renew our minds to the truth of His Gospel.

No matter how long it takes us, no matter how many times we find ourselves scuttling back into the shadows, we must grab our own leash and drag ourselves back into the light of the Word. We must do what it takes to reprogram our thinking, to shake off the nagging feeling that we've shown up for the prom in our pajamas and stand tall in the revelation that we are the best dressed creatures on the planet—robed from the inside out with the righteousness of God.

I'll shoot straight with you. It's not easy. It takes determination and endurance and lots of time spent meditating God's Word. But you can do it if you only will.

Just before this chapter was written, I reconnected with Ava. I hadn't talked to her for years but as we chatted on the phone, she told me she'd been thinking about me lately. Sorting through some old files, she'd come across her notes from our sessions. "Vikki," she said, "remembering your breakthrough made me wish you'd share your story with more people. There are so many who need to hear it."

Then she confided something that surprised me. She said that in her experience as a counselor, she'd seen relatively few people find the kind of freedom and victory that I did. She said many get a glimpse of it, begin to head that way, but they don't complete the journey. They give up too soon. They go back to their old patterns of thinking and behaving. And they end up the same way they began.

After our conversation, as I thought about what a tragedy that is, my mind wandered back to a rather shocking women's meeting I was a part of a few years back. The ladies who attended, although few in number, were the cream of the Christian crop. Mature believers, ministers, leaders in the Church, they floated into the room like butterflies, trailed by whiffs of perfume, carrying leather bound Bibles in manicured hands. Smiling and greeting each other, they assembled with the grace of women who seem to have been born in church.

Unfortunately for them, I had been appointed to lead the meeting. Even more unfortunate for them, I'd just emerged from my years of getting free and I was determined to help others come out of hiding.

I had to admit, however, as I looked around the room at the lovely heads of highlighted hair bowed for the opening prayer, that this group didn't appear to have much reason to hide. But then, who knows? I figured I might as well ask a few bold questions and see what happens.

I can't remember exactly what I said that started it all. I think I suggested that perhaps these kinds of meetings were too formal to be much fun. That maybe we should open up a little and be more real with each other. Maybe we should share things about ourselves that we usually don't say, give up a few secrets that would help us know and understand each other better.

I don't know what I expected to happen. Not much, I guess. I imagined we would break the ice in the first meeting by sharing the little things. Minor frustrations and struggles. Confessions like, "I hate to cook so much that my husband is threatening to build a house without a kitchen. He says he's tired of paying for wasted space." (That's a confession that in all honesty I could have made.)

But it's not the kind of thing these women said.

The first one got the ball rolling by admitting, with passion, just how much she detested meetings like these. She hated how phony everybody is. She resented the feeling of competition, with everybody boasting about how big their ministry is growing or how much success their church is having. It felt like a bunch of kids elbowing their way to the top of the heap in a religious game of King of the Mountain.

"Uh...okay. That's a good start," I said, wondering where to go next.

I didn't have to wonder long.

One by one, the ladies began to share their stories. Heart-breaking stories. Stories of abuse and shame and sadness. Some had been hiding those stories for decades, scared that if anyone found out, they'd be judged and rejected. Some had spent years working feverishly to overcome the ugly stains of their past. Just like I did, they'd been sewing fig leaves to cover up their sense of inadequacy. They'd been doing and doing in spite of the fact that, through Jesus, what they were trying to accomplish had already been done.

I don't mind telling you, I thought those women were awesome. They were as honest and courageous as any I'd ever met. But many of them were also weary. They needed someone to throw them the lifeline, the same one that Jesus threw to me when I was drowning in a sea of doing, too tired to swim another stoke.

Come into fellowship with me if you are tired and burdened and I will refresh and release you. Take the burden of responsibility I give you and thereby discover your life and your destiny. I am gentle and humble; I am willing to relate to you and permit you to learn at your own rate; then in fellowship with me, you will discover the meaning of life. My fellowship will release you and my companionship will direct you on your journey.

Matthew 11:28-30 BCJ

Or, as the King James Version translates it:

Come unto me, all ye that labour and are heavy laden, and I will give you rest. Take my yoke upon you, and learn of me; for I am meek and lowly in heart: and ye shall find rest unto your souls. For my yoke is easy, and my burden is light.

You shall find rest. That's what happens when we stop living in *do* and start living in *done*. We enter the rest that Jesus provided for us. When the revelation of His finished work makes the 18-inch journey from our head to our heart, we can finally relax. We can stop striving to be acceptable and simply enjoy being accepted. We can stop trying to earn our right standing with God and receive it instead as a gift.

We can become human beings instead of human doings.

Don't misunderstand. I'm not saying we won't work anymore for Jesus. I'm not saying we'll just sit around on our blessed assurance, eating bonbons and watching TBN. Not by a long shot.

Look again at the word *done* and you'll see that there's a *do* inside of it. Do you know what that means to me? It means that Jesus has divine assignments for each one of us. God-ordained mission impossibles that we can only complete as the grace of God empowers us to do what we would never be able to do on our own. Sadly, many believers are so busy performing that they totally miss their assignments. They never learn the difference between the two.

But there is a huge difference. Performance and assignment are as opposite as can be.

One is exhausting, the other exhilarating.

One is driven by fear, the other inspired by faith.

One is rooted in sin consciousness, the other in a revelation of righteousness.

Getting that revelation of righteousness is a process. It's not something that comes to us overnight. I've been working on it for many years now. I still have a lot to learn but when I think back to that starlit night on the bank of the Colorado River, I realize how far I've come.

Who could have imagined that the woman who once quaked with terror at the thought of sharing her testimony with a few ministerial rafting buddies would one day print the story of her past in a book for all to read? Who would have thought that she would tell her well-hidden secrets without feeling a trace of sadness or shame?

Jesus, that's who.

Because He knew long before I did that when I gave my life to Him, I became another person entirely. A person without a past. A new creation. A righteous child of Almighty God.

He knew that everything I was wearing myself out to achieve...had already been done.

CHAPTER 8

Good Morning, Lord

Now the Lord is the Spirit, and where the Spirit of the Lord is, there is liberty (emancipation from bondage, freedom). And all of us, as with unveiled face [because we] continued to behold [in the Word of God] as in a mirror the glory of the Lord, are constantly being transfigured into His very own image in ever increasing splendor and from one degree of glory to another; [for this comes] from the Lord [Who is] the Spirit.

2 Corinthians 3:17-18 The Amplified Bible

Very few people on the planet wake up in the morning feeling divine. Those who do, don't feel that way very long. Not if they own a mirror anyway.

Forget what you've seen in the movies. No real life human adult bounds out of bed with hair beautifully tousled, face glowing like the first blush of dawn, and breath fresh as spring. No Christian this side of eternity starts their day (or ends it, for that matter) radiating the full glory and perfection of the risen Christ.

Even morning people like me—people who like to drive before dawn and get jiggy with the Oldies while the rest of the world is hitting the snooze button—confront a face in the bathroom mirror each morning that looks imperfect, to say the least. Hair more terrifying than tousled. Face more blanched than blushing. And breath...well, let's not even go there.

I can only imagine how my mirror might answer if, first thing in the a.m., I ever dared ask the question made famous by the fairy tale: *Who's the fairest of them all?*

"I don't know, friend. But if you're it, the rest of the world's in trouble." That's what my mirror would probably say.

But so what?

Yours would too.

And we can both laugh about it because, as believers, no matter how we may look on the outside, we are awesome on the inside. We carry in our spirit the very image of Jesus. Someday, the fullness of His image in us is going to be revealed. When it is, we know we'll look fabulous in every way just like Jesus does because the Bible says that "when He is revealed, we shall be like Him, for we shall see Him as He is" (1 John 3:2).

Talk about something to look forward to! One of these days, we are going to be 100% glorified, head to toe, inside and out. From then on, we'll be absolutely stunning. All the time.

Meanwhile...we must put up with being less than stunning in some ways. We must accept the reality that as much as we aspire to be completely perfect, we are not. Although on the inside we are glorious manifestations of the finished work of Christ, on the outside we are still under construction and will be for the rest of our earthly lives.

This may seem like an obvious point. Yet we often forget it. We get the idea somehow that we should be perfect right now, today. When we find that we can't be, we react in one of two ways. We either drive ourselves harder to attain perfection. Or we let the shame of our imperfections drive us back into hiding. (Sometimes we do both.)

That's why, if we want to live free, we must not only understand our divine spiritual identity, we must also accept our humanity. We must stop berating ourselves for our imperfections, quit trying to hide our weaknesses and shortcomings, and realize that everyone on earth has them.

Everyone.

"But Vikki," you might say, "isn't there a verse in the Bible that tells us to be perfect, even as our Father in heaven is perfect?"

Yes, Jesus said those words in Matthew 5:48. But in the original language, *perfect* doesn't refer to being flawless or without error, it means to be mature or fully developed. So, in essence, Jesus was saying, *Grow up to behave like your spiritual Father! Keep learning and changing. Continue the process of developing and maturing so that you progressively think, talk, and act more and more like God.*

There's a big difference between being like God and behaving like Him. The *being* part is instant. It happens the moment we receive Jesus as our Savior when our spirit is recreated in God's image. Once our spirit is regenerated, the *being* part is done. The *behaving* part, however, is just getting started because our spirit isn't the only issue. We must also deal with our soul and body.

I realize this may seem like simple information but it's absolutely vital. You'd be amazed at what a difference it can make in your life if you'll keep these three facts clearly in mind:

- You *are* a spirit. That's your true identity. It's the real you. Your spirit is the part of you that's already been made perfect and divine, sometimes referred to in the Bible as "the hidden man of the heart" (1 Peter 3:4), or "the inner man" (Ephesians 3:16). Your spirit is what enjoys fellowship with God. It's the part of you He communicates with. At the moment you received Jesus as Lord, your spirit became righteous, holy, and as Christ-like as can be.

- You *have* a soul. It includes your mind, will, and emotions. Unlike your spirit, your soul wasn't automatically changed the moment you were born again. It must undergo a process of change that takes place as you renew your mind with the Word of God. Your soul is transformed, not all at once the way your inner man is, but over time as you grow in your knowledge of the Lord.

- You *live* in a body. It's like a suit you wear. It clothes the inner you (your spirit and soul) so that you can operate and express yourself in the physical world. The body has no independent life of its own. Genesis says that God *formed* it or molded it like clay out of the dust of the earth. It was totally inanimate until God breathed His Spirit into it and it came alive. When the spirit departs from the body, it becomes as lifeless as a cast off coat.

Here's why all this is important. If you don't understand it, trying to live the Christian life will drive you nuts. You'll either sit back expecting your reborn spirit to automatically change your life and be sorely disappointed; or you'll

160

approach Christianity like you would a self-improvement program. You'll dig through the Bible and come up with a long list of do's and don'ts. Then you'll try to become what the Bible says you should be by keeping all the rules. When you fail—which you will, repeatedly—you'll beat yourself up, apologize to God for being such a disappointment, and try again.

If you stick with it long enough, you'll eventually be so overcome by shame that you'll re-join Elliot under the bed and refuse to come out again.

How can I be so sure this will happen?

Because the Christian life is not a self-improvement program. It's not a behavioral modification plan that we enforce on ourselves. It's not a kind of clean-up campaign for our sin.

The Christian life is a process of regeneration. It starts *of the soul and body* with an impartation of the life and nature of God Almighty into the human spirit. It progresses as the believer's new, Godlike, God-indwelt identity works its way from the inside to the outside—from the hidden man of the heart into the soul which, in turn, reveals the new nature through the actions of the body.

This is the process of Christian growth that takes us from simply *being* like our Heavenly Father to actually *behaving* like Him. And, as I said, it's a process that continues all our life.

Arguing with the Holy Spirit

I got my first glimpse of how the process works not long after I was saved when my new spiritual nature started tampering with my attitudes about my mother. I can assure you,

I had no behavior modification program going in that area back then. I was not on a campaign to change my feelings toward her, sinful as they might seem.

The reality was, I hated her. And I expected to continue doing so.

If God had a problem with that I was truly sorry but I had no hope of changing it. My painful relationship with her had not just calloused the part of my soul that should have loved her, it had calcified it hard as rock. I wasn't proud of it but I wouldn't deny it either. I knew the truth and, shameful as it might be for a Christian to admit, I wasn't going to lie about it. Not to myself and not to God.

That being the case, you can imagine how I reacted when, a few months after I was saved, this instruction floated up from my heart to my mind. *Vikki, I want you to say, "I love my mother."*

When we are growing up in Jesus, we can be wildly wrong in one area and arrogantly right in another at the same time. That's how it was with me back then. I might have been hateful toward my mom, but I was determined not to be dishonest. So I fired back with what I thought was the truth.

"No! I won't say that. It would be a lie. I don't love my mother. I hate her."

At the outset, it didn't occur to me that I was arguing with the Holy Spirit. I assumed the strange idea had simply surfaced at random from the depths of my subconscious. So, after submerging it again, I turned my mind to other things.

Oddly enough, however, I found the thought resurfacing, like a bobber on a fishing line. Every time it was the same. *Vikki, say that you love your mother.*

As I considered it, my soul recoiled. My mouth clamped shut. *Why on God's green earth would I ever say such a thing? It would be a total fabrication and I'm not going to do it.*

The Holy Spirit is gentle but persistent. So the instruction tugged at my mind again. *Say you love your mother.*

"But I don't!" I protested. "I hate her. I can't help it. I wish I didn't but I do."

Say it anyway. It's not hard. Just open your mouth and say, "I love my mother."

I thought about it for a while, wondering what might happen if I did. I supposed it was possible that the Lord was trying to get something across to me. Perhaps this was a prompting of the Spirit and He had some valid reason for it. If so, I should at least try it.

"Okay. I love my mother."

Good. Say it again.

"I love my mother."

Strange. Even though my emotions denied the words, something inside me encouraged me to keep saying them. My spirit bore witness that in some way I didn't yet understand, I was actually telling the truth. So I stuck with it. Over the next weeks and months, each time I would think of it, I would say, "I love my mother."

The more I said the words, the easier it became. The more right they seemed. Until one day I made a shocking discovery. In spite of all that had happened in my childhood, in spite of all the mistakes my mother had made, I really did love her.

Some people might call that positive thinking. They might claim I'd talked myself into changing my feelings. But there was far more to it than that. What I did was renew my mind to reality; and this was the reality: The day I was born again, the love of God—His very own loving nature—was poured out into my heart by the Holy Spirit (Romans 5:5). His light dispelled the darkness within me and the hatred I'd long harbored for my mother fled.

It just took a while for my mind and my emotions to find out about it. They had to be renewed to the truth. One way to do that is with words. Although, I didn't know it back then, speaking a spiritual truth causes it to become fact in the natural world. So, as I obeyed the leading of the Holy Spirit, my soul found out (much to my surprise) what my spirit already knew—that in my heart of hearts, I truly did love my mom.

I'm happy to say that eventually my mother discovered it too. She must have been surprised, although she wasn't one to discuss such things. How could she have dreamed that when the years took their toll and she needed someone to lean on that I (of all people!) would count it an honor to care for her? How could she have imagined that I would be among those who lovingly watched over her in the sunset years of her life?

Without Jesus, it never could have happened. If He had not helped me grow up a little in Him, I would have missed the opportunity. I would never have gotten to say, with my voice and with my actions, the words that for so many years were left unspoken: *Mother, I love you.*

And I would never have known that, in the end, she loved me too.

Jesus Is Human Too

Considering how it began, my relationship with my mother ended—at least, until we meet again in heaven—amazingly well. It was nothing short of a miracle. But, that said, it was not perfect.

Because I'm not perfect.

And she wasn't perfect.

We were both works in progress—born-again human beings in the process of growing up into the likeness of God.

As Christians, that's what we all are.

At times, it can be aggravating to be so human. The growth process can seem agonizingly slow. But lest you get too bummed about it, here's something that will encourage you: Jesus is human too.

Granted, He's glorified now, seated at the right hand of God in a body that's eternal and imperishable, blazing with divine power; but He didn't have that advantage when He was on earth. Back then, He was as mortal as we are. Even though His spirit was divine, His soul was as human as ours, His body no more than a clay vessel of perishable flesh.

Most people forget that. When they read stories about Jesus in the Bible, they think He was so heavenly that His feet hardly touched the ground. They have the impression (gleaned, no doubt, from certain religious works of art) that Jesus floated a few inches above everybody else with a golden halo around His head. Nobody ever imagines Him getting dirty, or drowsy, or dealing with other all-too-human dilemmas. But the Bible makes it plain that He did.

165

It tells us that when He stopped at Jacob's well and talked to the Samaritan woman, He was weary from His journey and wanted a drink of water (John 4:5-7). It says He was so exhausted after ministering one day that He fell asleep in the boat afterward in the middle of a storm (Mark 4:38). It says that He got so hungry that He went to the fig tree looking for something to eat (Matthew 21:18). According to the Scriptures, Jesus was even tempted by the devil and had to resist him the same way we do—with the written Word.

"But Vikki, how could Jesus be human? He's God!"

Indeed, He is. He is all God and all man. He is as sovereign as the Eternal Father and as human as can be. It's hard for us to wrap our minds around this, but the Bible says that Jesus…

> …although being essentially one with God and in the form of God [possessing the fullness of the attributes which make God God], did not think this equality with God was a thing to be eagerly grasped or retained, but stripped Himself [of all privileges and rightful dignity], so as to assume the guise of a servant (slave) in that He became like men and was born a human being.
>
> Philippians 2:6-7, The Amplified Bible

This is the astounding truth. When Jesus became a man, He emptied Himself of all divine advantage. He limited Himself and became as human as any other man. Although He retained His righteous, holy nature, He laid aside all His divine powers and entered this world as a little baby, as weak and helpless as any other.

Those facts are central to the Gospel and we can never afford to forget them. If we do, we lose all hope that we can ever be like Jesus. We think of Him as having an unfair advantage over us. When we read in the Bible that He said,

166

"...he who believes in Me, the works that I do he will do also; and greater works than these he will do, because I go to My Father" (John 14:12), instead of believing and acting on His words, we roll our eyes and think, *Yeah, right, like that's going to happen.*

What's more, when we lose touch with Jesus' humanity, we lose patience with our own. We get frustrated with the growth process. Rather than enjoying Jesus' offer to relate to us and let us learn at our own rate, we wear ourselves out trying to be perfect. We expect to mature overnight and know everything about our life and destiny...right now.

If we'd just stop to think, we'd realize it's ridiculous. After all, even Jesus wasn't born spiritually mature. He didn't start out in life knowing everything. He didn't instantly become all He was destined and equipped by God to be. He had to discover who He was. He had to learn His true identity the same way you and I do—through the Word of God.

Like every other human being, Jesus had to develop by degrees as He fellowshipped with God and meditated the Word. His faith life increased incrementally, "...precept upon precept; line upon line, line upon line; here a little, and there a little" (Isaiah 28:10) much like we increase "from glory to glory" (2 Corinthians 3:18).

It always encourages me to remember that!

When I'm feeling like I still have a lot to learn, it cheers me up to think that even Jesus had to "grow and become strong, increasing in wisdom" (Luke 2:40 NASB). He didn't show up at the Temple at 12 years old, knowing all the answers. He sat among the teachers "both listening to them, and asking them questions" (v. 46). I'm glad that Jesus had to learn by asking questions because I do too.

Even after Jesus grew up and went into ministry, He dealt with human limitations. He didn't automatically know what to do in every situation. He had to seek God in prayer and get direction day by day. He had to continually fellowship with the Father to find out the details of His God-given assignment. Sometimes He had to pray all night long, like He did before appointing the 12 apostles (Luke 6:12-13).

It's easy for us to assume that Jesus had a special impartation from God that enabled Him to discern the leading of the Holy Spirit without effort. But He didn't. He had to develop in that area just as we do. He grew in His ability to hear and receive from God by study and practice. If He'd had some special ability that we don't have, He could have prayed for five minutes and gotten the answer every time. But that's not what happened.

In Gethsemane, He had to pray three times before He received what He needed. He even asked three of His disciples to help Him. They weren't much use, though. They fell asleep. So He pressed in all by Himself until, finally, He got the strength from God to fulfill His assignment at Calvary.

"Yeah, but you still have to admit that Jesus had extra power the rest of us don't have," somebody might say. "Just look at all the miracles He did."

According to Jesus, those miracles weren't done by His power but by His Father's. "Most assuredly, I say to you, the Son can do nothing of Himself," He said, "...the Father who dwells in Me does the works" (John 5:19; 14:10).

Jesus made such statements many times when He was on earth. He emphasized His humanity again and again. While He acknowledged His divinity and the fact that He was the Son of God, He most often referred to Himself as the Son of Man. To me, that's a big deal and here's why: Jesus is our example. If Jesus accepted His humanity, we can too. If He was patient with His growth process, we can be patient with ours. If He had to develop, discover and step into His destiny a little at a time, we can be content to do the same thing.

We can stop worrying about our weaknesses and trying to hide them, and get on with the business of growing up.

Adventures with Bonnie and Clyde

Truth be told, we can't hide our weaknesses anyway. Somebody always discovers them. I was reminded of that recently when I was telling someone about my spiritual journey. I'd just finished recounting the many splendid victories the Lord had given me. I'd shared how through Matthew 11:28-30, He taught me to take only the responsibilities He has given, how He helped me cast aside the perfectionist, people-pleasing, rescuing tendencies that had once held me captive...when I was confronted with what turned out to be a humbling question.

"Can you give me an example of the kind of thing you used to do before the Lord set you free?"

"Well..." I said, "let me think."

Digging desperately through my mental archives, I searched for some ancient anecdote I could tell on myself. I tried to come up with a story from years ago, some incident dating back even before my days in counseling. *Long ago, in a galaxy far, far away...* That's the way I would have liked to start. But nothing like that came to me. All I could think of was what I'd done just few days earlier.

Much as I hated to admit it, that very weekend in spite of all my progress over the past few years, I had stumbled into an old, familiar trap. *Give me a break*, I thought. *I don't want to tell this story. It's not even exciting. It's just the ordinary stuff of everyday life.* Which, of course, is why it was important for me to share it. Shrugging my shoulders, I plunged in...

The trouble had started during an innocent conversation with a good friend and fellow minister, whom I will charitably and incorrectly refer to as *Clyde*. We were chatting about some of his recent meetings when Clyde confided that something was bothering him. A person he highly esteemed (whom I will call Bonnie) hadn't come to hear him preach in quite some time. He felt disappointed and a little hurt by her absence.

Let me be clear. Clyde was not weeping and gnashing his teeth. He wasn't begging for me to save him from desolation and despair. He was simply telling me how he felt. All he wanted was a listening ear.

But I, Vikki Burke—Erstwhile Rescuer of Friends and Family—decided to fix the problem.

I took it upon myself to make sure that the next time Clyde stepped on the platform to preach, he would see Bonnie's face beaming back at him from the congregation.

Never mind that Clyde didn't ask me to intervene in the situation. Never mind that Jesus hadn't called me to fix things up between Bonnie and Clyde. I sprung to their rescue anyway. Why shouldn't I? I figured it would be easy.

It wasn't, of course. (Nothing done outside the will of God is ever easy.) I soon found out that there were actual reasons why Bonnie had been missing Clyde's services. She wasn't just neglecting him. She was awash with responsibilities and obligations that kept her away. She had her family to tend to, as well as ministry duties of her own. Thus, to complete my mission, I had to make arrangements for her responsibilities to be otherwise handled. Numerous phone calls and preparations had to be made. Plans had to be carried out. Primarily by me.

It turned out to be—as rescuing and fixing always does—quite a lot of work. But I persevered. Why? Because I was imagining how pleased Clyde would be when my plan succeeded. I was anticipating his "thank yous" and "you're so wonderful." I was aching for that people-pleasing pat on the back.

Problem is, I didn't get it.

Everything else went as I'd hoped. Clyde preached. Bonnie was there. But afterward, when I rushed up to receive my accolades, Clyde didn't even mention it.

So I did. Of course. I pointed out how great it was that she came to hear him. Wasn't he happy? Didn't that make him realize that she really did love and appreciate his ministry? And, by the way, I had a hand in the whole thing. Yes, it was difficult, a Herculean effort, but I made a way for her to be there...

Clyde looked at me as if he wished he could find a remote and press the *Mute* button. Then he changed the subject.

Hurt and disappointed, I huffed my way from the church sanctuary to the car. As my high heels clicked self-righteously across the pavement in the parking lot, I mentally muttered my indignation. Words like *ungrateful, see-if-I-ever-do-anything-for-you-again,* and *unappreciated* popped inside me, energized by the heat of the moment like corn kernels in a microwave.

If that was the end of the story, it would be a sorry one indeed. It would seem that all my years of Christian growth had come undone and I was aging backward, like Brad Pitt in *Benjamin Button*. But, thank God, that's not the end of the story.

Although I'm not perfect, I have made progress; and here's the proof: By the time I'd changed from my church clothes to my blue jeans, I recognized what I'd done.

I'd created the whole fiasco myself. Bonnie and Clyde weren't to blame for it. I was. I'd made the mistake of jumping into the middle of a situation I had no business being involved in. I'd taken on a responsibility not given to me by the Lord.

When it first hit me, I was tempted to feel like I do when I go to the mirror in the morning—like an imperfect mess. But then I thought about how much I've grown. I focused on the fact that, despite my mistake, rescuing is no longer a lifestyle for me. It has become the exception and not the rule.

Christian success isn't defined as perfection but as perpetual growth, and according to that definition, I'd ended my Bonnie and Clyde adventure as a success. Not everybody would see it that way. But the person I shared the story with that day did. Rather than being disappointed by my imperfection, she thanked me for my willingness to be real.

She walked away a little more comfortable with her humanity, and a lot more committed to making progress every day.

Mirror, Mirror...

What's the secret to making that kind of perpetual progress? It's simple as can be: Just keep looking in the mirror.

Not the mirror on your bathroom wall that reflects the temporal flaws and imperfections of your body. Not the mirror of circumstances and mistakes that reflects the immaturity of your soul. Another mirror altogether. The one that reveals the eternal beauty and perfection of your spirit. The mirror of the written Word of God.

Amazing things start to happen when you look at yourself daily in that wonderful mirror because it shows you who you really are. It gives you the power to change your soul and renew your mind so that you can behave on the outside like who you are on the inside. That's what makes the Bible so vital to us as believers. It's more than just a good book. "The word of God is full of living power" (Hebrews 4:12). That's why we should spend as much time reading and meditating on it as we can.

For Christians who are serious about growing up, studying the Bible isn't just a religiously right thing to do. It's not a spiritual duty we perform because God will be peeved at us if we don't do it. No! We treasure our time with the Scriptures because we know that those of us who continue "to behold [in the Word of God] as in a mirror the glory of the Lord, are constantly being transfigured into His very own image in ever increasing splendor and from one degree of glory to another..." (2 Corinthians 3:18, The Amplified Bible).

That alone is reason enough to spend time in the Word every single day. But there's another reason too.

The devil.

He has a mirror of his own that he is continually shoving in our face. Unlike God's mirror, the devil's magnifies our faults and failures. It blows every imperfection out of proportion. It deceives, discourages, and destroys.

Have you ever gone into the Fun House at an amusement park and seen the mirrors that mess with your reflection?

You look at yourself in one and you're tall and skinny. You look in another and you're short and fat. That's what the devil does. He makes amusement park mirrors out of experiences you've had and words spoken by significant people in your life. He takes even the most casual negative comments made by friends, a spouse, teachers or an employer and uses them to darken and distort your self-image.

His goal is to keep you trapped in sin-consciousness. To make you more aware of your fleshly weaknesses, faults, and failures than you are of the beautiful new creation you became when you got saved. He wants you to see yourself in a negative light and make you feel ashamed, inferior, inadequate, and deficient so that you'll think you're unworthy and shrink back from all that God has freely given you. He wants you to settle for being less than who you really are.

The devil knows, even if we don't, that sin consciousness is at the root of every spiritual failure. It allows us to mentally agree with the Bible and say we've been born again while keeping us stuck in the shameful feelings and behaviors of the past. It keeps us from growing and making progress in our Christian life.

The devil's mirror of sin-consciousness tricks us into thinking and acting like sinners even though we've been saved by grace.

But here's the good news.

You don't have to let the devil's stupid mirror bother you! You can treat it just like you do the ones at the park. You don't cry and get depressed when you look in those mirrors, do you? No, you laugh at them. You point at your skinny, stretched-out image, or your fat, squatty-looking image and say, "Ha! That's not me. I don't look like that at all."

How can you be so confident?

Because you have an accurate mirror at home that you look at multiple times a day. You know how you really look. And a thousand Fun House mirrors can't make you doubt it. The same thing can be true spiritually. In your Bible, you have a mirror that gives you an accurate reflection of your recreated spirit. It's designed to free you from sin-consciousness and make you righteousness-conscious. The more you look into that mirror, the more certain you'll be of who you really are. The more certain you become about who you are, the more your thoughts and actions will change, and the more you will grow up into the image of the Lord.

I do have to warn you, though; as human beings we're always in a hurry. So if the changes don't happen as fast as you want, you may be tempted to get discouraged. Instead of staying in the rest that Jesus offers and learning at your own rate, you may start fretting about your imperfections.

If you catch yourself doing that, stop. Relax and remember that growing up in Christ is a process that will continue all your life. Remind your fussy flesh that Christian maturity comes from "practice" (Hebrews 5:14 NASB) and then keep on practicing.

When you make a mistake or stumble into sin, don't give up on yourself. Just acknowledge that you missed it. Go to God and act on 1 John 1:9 which says, "If we confess our sins, He is faithful and just to forgive us our sins and to cleanse us from all unrighteousness." Then get back up, and start practicing righteousness again.

All the while, encourage yourself with the fact that God isn't focusing on your faults. He's looking at you through the perfection of Jesus. Even as He helps you grow, He's rejoicing over your right standing with Him. He is seeing the finished work of Christ in your spirit, the work of holiness and righteousness within you that's already been done. He is fully accepting you and loving you right now, just as you are.

How He does it, I can't say. All I know is that He does.

Somehow He is able to look beyond all the temporary imperfections in our soul and behold the eternal perfection in our spirit. He is able to enjoy the loveliness of our inner man even while outwardly we are still under construction. In our frumpiest moments—when we've just rolled out of bed and we're staring bleary-eyed into the bathroom mirror, toothbrush in hand—He can say to us in all sincerity, "Good morning, Beautiful."

And if we've been looking in the mirror of the Word, we'll be able to answer without a trace of shame and say, "Good morning, Lord."

CHAPTER 9

Saying Goodbye to the Blame Game

...God made you alive with Christ. He forgave all our sins. He canceled the record that contained the charges against us. He took it and destroyed it by nailing it to Christ's cross. In this way, God disarmed the evil rulers and authorities. He shamed them publicly by his victory over them on the cross of Christ. So don't let anyone condemn you...

Colossians 2:13-16

When I did it, I wasn't old enough to know I was playing out the classic human drama. I had no clue I was falling into a trap that was as old as Adam and Eve. All I knew was that my little brother had bullied me long enough...and it was time for him to pay.

So I bit myself on the arm. Hard.

It sounds insane, I realize, but I was just a kid at the time. Plus, there was method to my madness. Sporting a clear set of teeth marks, I ran to my parents, howling in pain, and blamed my brother.

They responded just as I'd hoped. Horrified by my report that their ruthless son had leapt on me like a grizzly and attempted to gnaw my arm to a nub, they sprung into action. Mom fetched my brother. Dad dragged out the belt. And, much to my delight, the whipping began.

I felt not one whit of regret as I listened to the thwamp of leather against my brother's behind. Not a single tear shimmered in my eye at his pitiful protests of innocence. So what if he had not committed this particular crime? My brother was guilty of plenty. He deserved to be punished.

I should know. I was his innocent victim.

I was the one he'd thrashed with a coat hanger and whipped with the garden hose. I was the one he chased down the street while brandishing a kitchen knife. He meant to stab me with it, too. If I hadn't dodged into a neighbor's house and locked myself in the bathroom, who knows what harm I might have suffered? I might not have even survived to see this day, to enjoy the exquisite justice that was finally being meted out to my brother.

Unaware of my mother's watchful gaze, I smiled to myself and relished the moment. My plan had unfolded so perfectly! I couldn't resist reliving it a little. Baring my teeth with jaw ajar, I pretended to repeat my stunt and see if I could match my teeth to the exact bite marks on my arm.

It was a bad idea.

Parents are always smarter than children think, so my mother already suspected that something wasn't quite right. All I did was provide the proof. What followed was a swift and tragic reversal of fortune. My mother informed my father that I was the bite-er as well as the bite-ee. My brother scampered away scot free. And I got the spanking.

If the punishment was meant to produce repentance in me, it failed. As I saw it, I'd simply been victimized by my brother one more time. Somehow, he'd turned the tables and made it appear that I was at fault. My parents might be fooled by the fact that the incisor indentions on my forearm were self-inflicted, but I knew the truth. In this situation, as always, my brother was to blame.

It was a lesson I learned well and used often. In my life as a perfectionist, I found that blame came in handy in all kinds of situations. It eased my feelings of inadequacy when I failed or made a mistake. It deflected my guilt when I did something wrong.

There was just one hitch. Although for years I didn't realize it, blame turned me into a victim. It put me in bondage and left other people in control of my life. Worst of all, blame stopped me from acknowledging my need for God's forgiveness, mercy, and grace. It stopped me from receiving the love and acceptance He was offering me.

Blame kept me imprisoned, even though God had made the way for me to be set free.

That's what blame always does. If you don't believe it, think again about what it did to Adam and Eve. They were the first ones ever to bite themselves and blame their brother. They introduced the blame game to the whole human race and people all over the planet have been playing it ever since.

To give credit where it's due, the devil is the one who initially got things rolling. He is, after all, "the accuser" of the brethren who accuses people before God day and night (Revelation 12:10). Blaming is intrinsic to his nature. So once Adam and Eve surrendered to him and fell under his influence, they immediately started pointing the finger of blame.

They didn't have to do it. The devil wasn't holding a gun to their head forcing them to cover their sin by blaming somebody else for it. They could have done something entirely different. They could have simply confessed and thrown themselves on God's mercy. I'm convinced that God could have spared them great pain if they'd just said, "God, You know everything! You know we've disobeyed you. You know we've sinned. We admit it. We take responsibility for this mess we've made. We don't know how to fix it. We don't have the power. But You do, so we ask You to forgive us and help us straighten things out. Help us get back into right standing with You."

We'll never know exactly what would have happened if they'd said those things because they didn't. They played the blame game instead...and lost big time.

When God asked Adam, "Have you eaten the fruit I commanded you not to eat?" Adam admitted what he'd done but blamed Eve for it. "...it was the woman you gave me who brought me the fruit, and I ate it," he said (Genesis 3:11-12).

Actually, Adam's accusation not only made Eve the scapegoat for his sin, it laid the blame on God as well. Adam as much as said, "As long as I was alone, I was immovable in my integrity and allegiance. But then *You* gave me the woman. I wouldn't have done this if she hadn't come on the scene. You and Eve set me up. You're both against me. You're the ones who are guilty. I'm just a victim."

Can you imagine taking such an attitude toward God?

Yes, you can. So can every other human being, because at one time or another we've all done it. We've all blamed God for the trouble in our life. We might not have been bold or foolish enough to accuse Him out loud right to His face like Adam did, but in our hearts, we've passed the buck to Him.

We've blamed Him for things like sin, sickness, negative circumstances, and financial lack; and then we've put a pious face on it by saying things like, "Well, I guess God just sent these bad things into my life to teach me something. He put this sin in my path to help me stay humble."

I don't care how religiously right that may sound, the Bible says it's wrong. It tells us very plainly: "When someone is tempted, he shouldn't say that God is tempting him. God can't be tempted by evil, and God doesn't tempt anyone. Everyone is tempted by his own desires as they lure him away and trap him" (James 1:13-14, God's Word Translation).

God doesn't have it in His nature to tempt people to sin; and He doesn't go into partnership with Satan to teach us things. He doesn't buddy up with sickness, poverty, and trouble which are all the foul offspring of the curse of sin and put them on us to strengthen our faith. If those things strengthened faith, the world would be absolutely full of spiritual giants.

What God uses to instruct us is the Word! Second Timothy 3:16 says:

All Scripture is inspired by God and is useful to teach us what is true and to make us realize what is wrong in our lives. It straightens us out and teaches us to do what is right. It is God's way of preparing us in every way, fully equipped for every good thing God wants us to do.

Temptation is not our teacher. The devil's stuff—whether it's doubt, sickness, poverty, or any other evil thing—is not our strengthener. Trouble is not what equips us to do God's will. God has given us the Bible and the Holy Spirit to teach us and help us grow up in Him. He is our helper, not our tempter. So never blame God for what's gone wrong in your life. Wherever there is a falling short, never look God-ward. Don't make the mistake that some people do who "ruin themselves by their own stupid actions and then blame the Lord" (Proverbs 19:3 TEV). Instead, look inward. Ask yourself and God, "Did I miss something? Lord, show me where I got off course."

Obviously, that's not what Adam did. He stood there in his fig leaf bloomers and blamed God for his fall. He said, "At the root of it, this is all Your fault!"

It's a testimony to divine patience and love that Adam survived the conversation. God could have justifiably fried him like a strip of bacon right on the spot. But God wasn't out to fry His fallen children; He was out to forgive them. He wanted to redeem them from their predicament, not punish them for it.

Adam passed up that opportunity, however, by passing the blame instead of repenting and taking responsibility. So God turned his attention to Eve. Without responding at all to what Adam said, God submitted the question to her and gave her the opportunity to make a different choice.

"How could you do such a thing?" He asked.

For a split second, hope glimmered in the Garden. Eve, caught with fruit juice still dripping down her chin, made no attempt to deny her actions. The evidence of her guilt was too plain for a plea of innocence. But, like her husband, Eve had been infected by the spirit of accusation. So she too passed the blame.

"The serpent tricked me," she replied. "That's why I ate it."

It's easy to imagine that God and all the hosts of heaven sighed with disappointment when they heard those words. Eve's accusation, her blame-shifting, proved once and for all that the first couple had gone renegade. They had aligned themselves with the devil and were now following his twisted guidance, heeding his dark counsel.

All of heaven knew that if the light of God had still illuminated Adam and Eve's hearts, they never would have blamed each other. They would have done just the opposite. They would have interceded for each other before God. They would have made allowances for each other's faults. That's God's nature and it's what He always leads His children to do. "Be patient with each other," He says, "making allowance for each other's faults because of your love" (Ephesians 4:2).

Have you ever noticed how much patience parents often have with the behavior of their little ones? If their baby is crying and creating a disturbance, they say, "Please forgive him. He didn't get his nap today. He's teething. He's hungry." They excuse the child's noisy wails because they love him. If somebody else's child is crying, however, the same parents often have an entirely different reaction. Suddenly, the crying is not the precious expression of a little one in distress; it's evidence that the kid is spoiled and needs discipline.

We make allowances for those we love. But sin stops the love. It stops us from receiving it; and it stops us from giving it. That's why a sin-conscious Christian:

- points the finger of accusation when someone does wrong

- feels the need to assign blame for every failure

- is conditioned to think that someone must pay

- seeks to identify and punish the guilty

183

- hopes to clear himself by pointing to others but can never escape the sense that he too is guilty and deserves to be condemned

Those are the deadly effects of sin-consciousness. Adam and Eve were the first to experience them but they weren't the last. We've all followed in their footsteps. We've all pulled up a chair to the table of sin and played a few rounds of the blame game.

Making the Hard Choice

When I set my sights on getting free from perfectionism, people-pleasing and the other traps I'd fallen into, I saw this right away: I could no longer afford to play the game. If I wanted to live the abundant life Jesus provided, I had to quit blaming others for the problems in my life and take responsibility for them myself. I had to quit giving other people control over me by seeing myself as a victim.

"But Vikki," somebody might say, "you *were* a victim! You had a very tough childhood."

Perhaps. But then, so did Joseph. My troubles pale in comparison to his. The Bible tells us that he was mistreated by his family in unthinkable ways. His brothers not only hated him, they plotted his murder. The only reason they didn't carry out their plot was because they decided it would be more profitable to sell him into slavery. Now, *that's* a dysfunctional family!

Joseph's trouble didn't stop there either. As a slave, he worked hard and served his employer loyally—only to be falsely accused of a crime and thrown into prison. Read his story in Genesis sometime. You'll see that if anybody had a right to a victim mentality, Joseph did.

But he refused to adopt that mentality. He never allowed the betrayal and mistreatment he experienced to turn him into a victim. He rose above it. He focused on the dream God put in his heart and kept his attitude pure toward those who had abused him.

I don't deny the reality of victimization. Many people suffer terrible pain through no choice or fault of their own. They experience abuse for which they are in no way responsible. But there comes a point for all of us where, if we want to be free, we must take responsibility for what we are doing today and begin the process of healing.

As long as we blame others for our failures, we give them power over our lives that God never meant them to have. We're falling for the devil's lie when we say to ourselves, "That person made me unhappy. He made me feel or act this way. He's the reason for my misery." The truth is that God has given each of us control of our own decisions, feelings, and actions. We may not be able to choose our circumstances, but we each have the power to choose our response to them. We can either make right choices and live happy, fulfilling lives; or we can make wrong choices and cause ourselves further needless pain.

God said it this way in Deuteronomy 30:19-20:

Today I have given you the choice between life and death, between blessings and curses. I call on heaven and earth to witness the choice you make. Oh, that you would choose life, that you and your descendants might live!

Choosing life over death seems like a no-brainer, but it's not. In fact, when it comes to blaming others for our failures or taking responsibility for them ourselves, few of us these days have the courage to make the right choice. That's why I was so inspired a few years ago when I read the story of Commander Scott Waddle. Unlike most of us, Commander Waddle was forced to make his choice in a very public way— in front of a court of inquiry commissioned by the United States Navy, with people all over the world waiting to hear what he would say.

Here's what happened: On February 9, 2001, Scott Waddle had been involved in a fatal accident. A nuclear submarine under his command, the USS Greeneville, had collided with a small Japanese fishing ship, the Ehime Maru. Nine people were killed, four of them high school students.

In his book, *The Right Thing*, the commander recounts the events that led to the collision. He acknowledges how tempted he was to claim he was a victim of someone else's mistakes. He tells how much he would have liked to explain that others should also be blamed for what happened.

How easy it was to mumble to myself, 'Hey, this was not my fault. The fire control technician had the information and the solution on his computer and could see it in front of him, but he didn't give it to me. It's his fault.' Although the information was there, I wasn't challenged when I said there were no visual contacts.[5]

But those are not the statements Scott Waddle made at the inquiry. He took full responsibility for the accident, against the counsel of his attorney and the Navy's direction. "There's a time to be silent, and a time to speak up for what

---

[5] Scott Waddle, *The Right Thing* (Brentwood, Tennessee: Integrity Publishers, 2002) p. 194.

186

is right," he says. "I had to take responsibility and let the chips fall where they may. It's the right thing to do."[6]

Right? Yes.

Easy? No.

Scott Waddle had spent years working his way up the ladder of the U.S. Navy. He'd worked hard to achieve an honor attained by only a select few—the command of a nuclear submarine. By taking others' advice and blaming his crew members, he could have salvaged his career. But in the process, he would have lost his self-respect, his family's admiration, a nation's trust, and most of all, his integrity. Those were the losses he could not bear.

So he made the hard choice. He didn't attempt to evade his responsibility or to redefine the word *responsible*. He simply opted out of the blame game.

It's one thing to admire such a man; it's another to follow his example. To do the latter, we must ask what gave him his courage. Commander Waddle himself gives the answer. He says that several things sustained him throughout the ordeal, including the unconditional love of family and the help of his friends.

But here's what he puts at the top of the list: his faith in God.

A Little Bit of Faith…and a Whole Lot of Fear

To those of us who know the Lord, that's not surprising. We know how crucial faith in Him can be in such situations. But we also have to admit that our faith doesn't always seem to give us the guts Scott Waddle had. Sometimes when we

---

[6] Ibid, caption in photo section.

make mistakes—mistakes less serious than his—we start pointing fingers of blame so fast and in so many directions that we look like windmills in west Texas.

It's not that we don't want to do what's right. We'd like to take responsibility for our blunders, but the truth is we're scared. Scared that the punishment might be more than we could bear. Scared that if we admitted we were wrong, we'd be judged permanently unworthy. Scared that the long arm of God's law will make us pay—and pay dearly—for what we've done.

I know very well what that kind of fear is like. I lived with it for years as an adult. But it made its entrance into my life long before then.

The first time I remember running into it head-on, I was a 12-year-old kid barreling down the street in my brother's brand new go-cart. The fear didn't come because I wrecked the cart, if that's what you're thinking (although that would have inspired plenty of fear, for sure). On the contrary, I was quite the excellent driver that day. Buzzing around the neighborhood like a pint-sized Danica Patrick, I whizzed past sedans and station wagons like they were sitting still. (Which, of course, they were because they were parked along the curb.)

What a glorious experience it was! Gasoline-scented wind in my hair. Steering wheel vibrating beneath my grip. Engine roaring like a lawnmower in my ears. Pavement streaking by at a dizzying 22 miles an hour. Everything was perfect... until I saw my father standing in the street a few yards in front of me, muscular arms akimbo, dark eyes flashing with fury, glaring directly at me.

My foot recoiled from the accelerator. Clearly I was in big trouble.

As I coasted to a stop, my thoughts raced back through the events of the day. A few hours earlier when my father had presented the go-cart to my brother for his birthday, he had forbidden any of us to drive it around the neighborhood. The reason was obvious. The cart was little more than a fragile metal frame with a motor. It was a fraction of the size of any other vehicle on the road. Driving it in traffic would be dangerous. "What's more, driving it on the street is illegal," my dad had explained. "You have to wait until we can take it to a track."

If you're a parent, you know what happened next. The begging commenced. My brother, his friends, and I bounced around my dad yipping and yapping like a bunch of pups. Our pleas were pitiful and persistent. "Please, Dad. Pleeeze! Just let us drive it to the end of the block and back. Please..."

As our relentless cries rained down on my father, his resolve began to melt. "Okay, you can drive the cart to the end of this block only. Then you must turn around and come back."

My brother went first. Obeying my father's exact instructions, he drove to the end of the block, then turned around and came back. Next, each of his friends took a turn, every one following his lead. To the end of the block and back. Just like Dad said.

Then came my turn. Heart skittering with excitement, I climbed into the little cart, revved the engine, and took off for the end of the block. I intended to turn around when I got there. Really, I did. But I arrived quicker than I expected and found myself not yet ready relinquish my exquisite ride.

So I kept going. Past the end of the first block to the end of the second. *Dad wouldn't mind*, I reasoned, *and he can't really see me anyway because the cars parked along the curb hide me from view*. At the end of block two, another thought occurred to me. *Instead of turning and going back, why shouldn't I just continue on around the block and make a big circle?* It seemed like a logical choice at the time, not to mention it would extend my ride a little more, so that's what I did.

I had just finished my loop and headed into the home stretch toward our driveway when I encountered Dad in his Mr. Clean stance. *Uh-oh*. Truth be told, I wasn't surprised I was in trouble. I knew I'd improvised on his instructions. But surely my slight transgression didn't merit the kind of severity I now saw on my father's face as he looked not just at me but beyond me...behind me...at something else...

Ratcheting my head toward the rear of the cart, my eyes caught the flash of red and blue lights, then the black and white of a police car. My skittering heart skidded to a stop. My short life passed before my eyes. The end had come. I had no idea what the police planned to do. Jail me, most likely. But it didn't really matter. They'd never get the chance. My dad would kill me first. He'd whale me to death with the spike studded belt he so often warned us about. My brother and I had never seen it but we felt sure it existed and today it would be my demise.

Drenched with dread, I stood barely conscious amid a blur of dark uniforms, silver badges, holstered guns, and the bass tones of male voices. Police asking questions. Dad answering. A citation being scribbled out. Something said about a court date. Dad stuffing the citation in his pocket. The black and white cruiser gliding slowly away. And Dad turning his back on me without a word.

I never got a spanking that day. Maybe the fear and remorse on my face sparked my father's mercy. I don't know.

He didn't speak to me for days afterward. His silence not only crushed me, it left me wondering if and when the beating might come. Either way, I knew that I still had to face the long arm of the law.

The day my father accompanied me to court began as one of the worst of my life. On the outside, I looked like any other 12-year-old girl as I trudged up the courthouse steps. But on the inside, I wore an orange prison uniform and shuffled along in manacles. *Guilty*—that's what I was, and every step brought me closer to punishment. I imagined iron bars clanking shut, a skeleton key turning in the lock, the guard's footsteps echoing down a cement hall, receding until I was left alone in silence. In jail. Where I deserved to be.

The courtroom looked just as I expected. Walnut paneled walls surrounded rows of oak benches facing a massive judicial desk. A black-robed judge frowned and examined documents handed to him by a clerk. Slamming down his gavel, the judge declared the court in session and barked out my name.

I stepped to the front of the courtroom, trembling like a paint shaker while the judge glowered down at me with fiery eyes. Ignoring my father who stood beside me, he ordered me to explain my crime. "Were you driving a go-cart on the street?" he said.

"Yes, sir, I was."

"And do you know that is illegal?" he snapped.

I opened my mouth...but I never got the opportunity to answer.

191

What happened next, I'm convinced I'll remember for all eternity. My father took a step forward, put his strong arm around my shoulder and pulled me behind him. He took my place in front of the judge. "Your Honor," he said, "It was my fault. I allowed her to drive the go-cart. I take full responsibility."

Stunned, relieved, and bewildered, I hid behind my father and marveled that he would take the blame for my wrongdoing. This wasn't his fault. I had disobeyed him. I had abused the privilege he had given me. I deserved to suffer the penalty. But I never did. Impossible as it seemed, I had acknowledged my trespass, taken responsibility for my crime, and yet I was never required to pay the price for it. Because of the merciful intervention of my father, the judge simply gave me a warning and let me go free.

What a vivid picture that was of what God has done for us!

Through the cross of Christ, He has stepped in front of us and taken responsibility for our sin. He has answered the demands of justice by taking our place and receiving the punishment we deserved. He has put His strong arm around us, hidden us behind His mighty love, and said, "I will take the blame for all you have done. I will pay the price with the blood of My own sinless Son. I will bear your guilt and set you free."

Guilt Is Never Good

This marvelous intervention by our Heavenly Father is what gives us the courage to resign the role of victim. It's what frees us from the fear of acknowledging our sins, short-comings, and failures. This is what gives us the guts to take responsibility for our actions, even when those actions fall far short of perfection: Understanding that we have nothing to be scared of. Our penalty has already been paid. Almighty God has declared us *Not Guilty*.

Before we were even saved, before we cried out for mercy when we were still in rebellion, God sent Jesus to die on our behalf and "...forgave all our sins. He canceled the record that contained the charges against us. He took it and destroyed it by nailing it to Christ's cross" (Colossians 2:13-14).

Think of it! Jesus has removed your name from any and all records that connect you with sin. Your name has been cleared. Your guilt has been forever expunged. Your history has been wiped clean. There is no evidence that you were ever identified with a crime. You can turn your back on the Accuser of the Brethren and walk out of the courtroom free. You don't have to let anyone burden you with blame ever again. If you do something wrong, you can admit it, receive your forgiveness, and make the necessary corrections. But you don't have to allow anyone to saddle you with guilt.

Guilt has absolutely no place in the life of a believer. It's a destructive emotion. It tears you down, damages your sense of personal significance, and causes self-condemnation. Guilt withers your spirit and produces fear of punishment. It says, "Now you're going to get it!" Instead of drawing us to God to receive His forgiveness and grace, guilt makes us feel too ashamed to face Him. It makes us see ourselves as such low-down, dirty, rotten, good-for-nothing sinners, that we want to throw our hands in the air and say, "I can never change! Why should I bother trying?"

Granted, some guilt-ridden people do keep trying for a while. They muster their determination and attempt to overcome their guilt by doing good deeds. But they always fail. They always end up feeling like they can never do enough to compensate for their shortcomings (which is true because the Bible says, "...by grace are ye saved through faith; and that not of yourself: it is the gift of God").[7] So they end up feeling guiltier still, and falling prey to depression, despair, and ultimately more sin.

I realize that many misguided Christians think that guilt can be used for good in their lives. Numerous parents, preachers, and teachers believe that it can be used as a powerful motivator. But they're wrong. Guilt can never inspire us to live for God. It's the product of sin. It's a tool of the enemy and there isn't a shred of good in it.

Every believer needs to settle this fact once and for all: Guilt is not from God. Ever.

"But Vikki," you might say, "how will we know that we're doing something wrong if we never feel guilty?"

The Holy Spirit will reveal it to us. He has the ability to convict us of sin without condemning us for it. His conviction encourages us to run to God rather than away from Him. It inspires us to ask Him to help us make the necessary changes in our lives so that we can fulfill His plan for us.

Guilt and conviction are worlds apart. They have two different authors. The Lord is the author of conviction; Satan is the author of guilt and condemnation.

Although Jesus bore our guilt and freed us from it once and for all on Calvary, the devil continues to try to trick us into accepting it. He attempts to pass it off as a counterfeit of conviction. But don't accept that counterfeit. Instead, stand on Romans 8:1-2 that says "There is therefore now no condemnation [a.k.a. guilt] for those who are in Christ Jesus.

[7] Ephesians 2:8

194

For the law of the Spirit of life in Christ Jesus has set you free from the law of sin and of death" (NASB).

The Phillips Translation of that verse says, "...there is no accusing voice nagging those who are united to Jesus!" So every time a nagging, accusing voice brings up your list of offenses, take your hammer and nail the list to the cross. Say, "Jesus bore those offenses and the guilt that went with them, so they have nothing to do with me!" Then, turn your attention away from the devil's accusations and focus instead on the unconditional love and acceptance of God. Spend time praising the Lord and meditating on the righteousness He has given you in Christ Jesus.

As you do that, you'll learn the same lesson a friend of mine did when she went to work as a teller for a bank. During her first week of training, she handled money all day long, every day. She counted it, sorted it, made change with it, touched it, and looked at it. On the last day of the week, her supervisor slipped a counterfeit bill into the mix. Do you know what happened? She recognized the counterfeit the moment she touched it. She'd become so familiar with the real currency that she couldn't be duped by the fake.

The same thing can happen to you spiritually. The more you focus on what's true and real according to the Word of God, the better you'll become at identifying and rejecting the devil's counterfeit. The more conscious you become of your righteousness, the harder it will be for the devil to pawn off his guilt on you.

Does that mean he'll stop trying? No. Regardless of how hard you make it for him, the devil will never give up. He'll keep doing his best to force his forgeries on you. When he does, resist him and he will flee from you (James 4:7). Open your mouth and remind the devil of the fact that Jesus' blood has cleansed you from all sin and all unrighteousness. Deal with him the same way the saints did in Revelation 12:10-11. When "the accuser" came against them, "they overcame him by the blood of the Lamb and by the word of their testimony."

Also, be sure to ask the Holy Spirit to help you recognize and cast down the thoughts that produce guilty feelings in you. Then be diligent to bring those thoughts "into captivity to the obedience of Christ" (2 Corinthians 10:5). Stubbornly refuse to believe the lies of the devil any longer. Choose to think only on things that are good, pure, lovely, and of a good report (Philippians 4:8).

Waiting to Exhale

I've said it before and I'll say it again, this isn't easy. It takes commitment and determination to walk continually in the grace and forgiveness of God, to shake free of guilt and condemnation, and to put an end to the blame game. But we must do it because it's the oxygen of Christianity. It's as essential as breathing and works much the same way: We draw God's forgiveness and grace into ourselves by faith in Jesus...then we release it by giving it to others.

Receive...give.

Receive...give.

Inhale...exhale.

All of us at times will catch ourselves waiting to exhale. When others hurt us, we'll be tempted to keep blaming them, to withhold from them the forgiveness that Christ has given to us. But that is deadly. It's like holding our spiritual breath. It not only deprives our offenders of the oxygen of divine life, it deprives us as well. It leaves us floundering, gasping for more of God's grace, yet mysteriously unable to breathe it in.

I know what that's like because I held my breath in one area of my life for almost 30 years. That's how long it took me to fully forgive my mother's boyfriend. The man I began to hate as a lost, grief-stricken 16-year-old. The man who moved into my house just weeks after my father's death. The man who forced his way into my family and refused to leave until the day he died.

To be clear, I didn't hate him the whole time. After I got saved and the Holy Spirit began His transforming work in my life, He helped me move gradually beyond my own pain and anger. He opened my eyes to the guilt, shame and misery that both my mother and her boyfriend had suffered. He helped me to some extent, at least, to have compassion for them.

But even so, where the boyfriend was concerned, I didn't fully exhale until he was about to die. That's when the Lord gave me a vision. In it, I saw my hands extended in front of me cupped together as if I was holding something. When I looked to see what it was, I realized it was this man's heart. Then I heard the Lord's voice inside me. *Vikki, you have the power to crush his heart and allow him to continue suffering the guilt and shame of his sin; or you can forgive him and release him from the prison of his lifelong bondage.*

The thought astonished me. Was it truly possible that I could have such an impact on another person's soul? Did I really possess the keys that would open his prison doors and set him free?

I knew in an instant the answer was *yes*. Jesus said so Himself. He breathed on His disciples after His resurrection and said, "Receive the Holy Spirit. If you forgive anyone his sins, they are forgiven; if you do not forgive them, they are not forgiven" (John 20:23 NIV).

What a decision I faced! This man had caused me years of pain. He'd done me great wrong at one of the cruelest times of my life. Surely, he didn't deserve to be forgiven. But then… neither did I. Yet God had pardoned me. Could I refuse to offer someone else the divine gift I had so freely received?

No, I couldn't. I wouldn't. So I chose to breathe.

I forgave the man completely. I released him from blame. I chose to hold nothing against him anymore. When I did, we both inhaled the very atmosphere of heaven. We both became more alive.

To be honest, I probably gained more than he did. By holding onto my accusations against this man, I'd allowed some of the devil's junk to cling to me. I'd missed out on a measure of God's grace in my life. When I forgave, I opened the door for it to flow more freely and abundantly than ever before and I've been determined ever since to keep that door open. If I'm tempted to hold something against someone who has hurt me or judge them for some wrong they've done, I just remind myself of Jesus' warning: "Judge not, that you be not judged. For with what judgment you judge, you will be judged; and with the measure you use, it will be measured back to you" (Matthew 7:1-3 NKJV).

This is the humbling truth. None of us can see clearly enough to judge the splinter of sin in our brother's eye; our vision is too badly obscured by the redwood-sized timbers in our own. That's why God in His great wisdom didn't assign any of us to be His agents of judgment. Jesus is the only One worthy of that task. So we will do well to mind our own business and leave the sins of others in His capable and merciful hands.

We know in advance, of course, what He will do about them—indeed, what He has already done by taking our place in court and shedding His blood to set us free. He will reach out to every trembling, shame-drenched soul that's been caught in sin the same way He reached out to the woman caught in adultery. When the religious leaders dragged her—all guilty and humiliated—into His presence, accusing her and demanding that He make her pay the penalty for her sin, He wouldn't do it.

As the only innocent One in the bunch, He had every right to judge her. He had every right to sentence her to death. But He relinquished that right. He refused to accuse or blame her, and stopped others from doing so by uttering one simple sentence. "He that is without sin among you, let him first cast a stone at her" (John 8:7).

> *Then those who heard it, being convicted by their conscience, went out one by one, beginning with the oldest even to the last. And Jesus was left alone, and the woman standing in the midst. When Jesus had raised Himself up and saw no one but the woman, He said to her, "Woman, where are those accusers of yours? Has no one condemned you?" She said, "No one, Lord." And Jesus said to her, "Neither do I condemn you; go and sin no more."*
>
> John 8:7, 8-11

Jesus didn't condemn that dear woman caught in adultery...and He doesn't condemn us. He takes our place, instead. He puts His strong arm around us, steps in front of us, and covers us with His own righteousness. He puts an end to stone-throwing with His mighty forgiveness and grace so that we can leave blame behind and get on with the business of breathing.

CHAPTER 10

Take Charge of the Camp

There is no fear in love; but perfect love casts out fear...
1 John 4:18

Mr. Duce was more like the Lone Ranger than an ordinary elementary school teacher. At least, that's what I thought. He didn't wear a black mask or ride a white stallion—he wore high-waisted slacks, a skinny tie, and drove a sedan—but he hi-ho-Silvered into my third grade year and became my hero just the same. Rescuing me briefly from fear's evil grip, he gave me one glorious day of freedom.

He came up with his plan a few months into the school year. Concerned to see me cowering in his classroom day after day silent as a shadow, he'd repeatedly tried to draw me out. When nothing worked, he called my mother about it. "Your daughter has never once spoken in class," he said. "I want to help her. What could I use to inspire her to talk? Is there anything in particular that interests her?"

Mother, who shrugged off my silence as nothing more than a silly case of shyness, mentioned the only thing that came to mind. "Well...we have a brand new litter of kittens," she said.

The next morning, at Mr. Duce's request, I arrived at school toting a bulky, blanket-lined cardboard box. Jostling around inside it were one mother cat and her four-week-old kittens. I wasn't sure why my teacher wanted my classmates to see them. Although I never tired of petting and playing with the never-ending stream of meow-meisters that leapt and tumbled through our house, they weren't exactly an endangered species. They were just ordinary kittens, plentiful as dandelions in spring and, according to my father, far less desirable.

Mr. Duce knew this, of course. But he also knew a few other things—including how my fellow students would respond. He suspected that when I showed up at school with pets in tow, for one shining moment, my little cats would make me the big dog.

Sure enough, it happened. As I sat on the wooden steps outside the classroom with my cardboard box waiting for the school bell to ring, the other students crowded around. Eager hands reached out and all eyes turned toward me. "Are these your kittens, Vikki?... How old are they?... Can I hold one? Please, can I?"

For the first time in my school career, I was the center of attention. Handing out kittens first to one child, then to another, the thrill of my classmates' approval buoyed me to new heights. Fear lost its stranglehold on me. "Yeah, they're my kittens all right. They're four weeks old. We always have kittens at our house. My mom loves them but they drive my dad crazy. Here, you can hold this one…Be gentle, okay?"

Usually when the school day started, Mr. Duce insisted we come inside and promptly get to work. But not that morning. The day I brought the cats to school, he let us huddle around them on the classroom steps long after the morning bell rang. He didn't make a big deal about it. He just watched, patient and smiling, as chattering children took turns cradling kittens in their arms and I presided over them all.

What an unforgettable day! I wanted it to last forever.

It didn't, of course. Twenty-four hours later, my new-found craving for approval set me up for a fall.

Our class was practicing penmanship when it happened. Seated at our desks with backs curved and heads bowed over our writing tablets, we etched the letters of the alphabet. At the front of the room, Mr. Duce rustled through homework papers at his desk, marking them with a red pen. Serenity reigned in the classroom. Life was good.

Then, tragically, I was stricken with an idea that before the kitten incident would have never occurred to me. I decided to show Mr. Duce my work.

What inspired me to do so was the masterful, cursive letter "J" I had crafted. It looked so lovely I felt sure it would elicit exclamations of approval from my teacher. So, putting down my yellow #2 pencil and picking up my tablet, I walked to his desk and spoke to him. Right out loud. For the first time ever.

For a few precious seconds it seemed like a good decision. Mr. Duce welcomed my interruption with enthusiasm and extolled the virtues of my "J." My scrawny ribcage began to inflate with self-esteem. Then I heard the titters of classmates who, overhearing Mr. Duce's praise, found my eagerness to please amusing. Here and there across the room, snickers broke out until the entire room roiled with laughter. All of it directed at me. Face burning with humiliation, ribcage deflated, I crumpled my "J" and returned to my chair in silence. I never opened my mouth in class again.

It was a long fall for a third grader—going from Kitten Cum Laude to Class Laughingstock overnight—and it hurt. I never blamed Mr. Duce for my pain, however. In my book he was and always will be a hero for what he tried to do. But the odds were stacked against him. His valiant attempt to save me from the fear of rejection was bound to fail.

The roots of that fear are too deeply entrenched in all of us to be dug up by human effort. Like shame, blame, and guilt, fear goes all the way back to the Garden of Eden. It's a primal force of evil generated and perpetuated by the devil himself. A force that reared its ugly head in the first sentence Adam spoke to God after the fall:

"I heard Your voice in the garden, *and I was afraid...*"

People who say that a little fear is a good thing are as wrong as they can be. It's a demonic killer. It's the prison the devil uses to keep people enslaved, and from the time it made its appearance on earth, God went to war against it. From Genesis onward, He commanded His people again and again to *fear not.*

God knows, even if we don't, that fear is always destructive. So even before He heard the first twinge of panic in Adam's voice, He came up with a plan to break its power. He foreordained the sending of a True Lone Ranger. An eternal Hero who would "...deliver and completely set free all those who through the [haunting] fear of death were held in bondage throughout the whole course of their lives" (Hebrews 1:14 AMP). A firstborn Son who would save His Father's quivering, shivering children from the world's ultimate terrorist, not with something as simple as a box of kittens, but by laying down His life.

The High-Octane Fuel of Fear

The fear that followed me back to my desk as an eight year old in Mr. Duce's class may sound like kid stuff, but let me assure you, it's not. It's one of the most pervasive and powerful of all fear's manifestations, the first fear that mankind ever confronted: the fear of rejection, the terrifying prospect that the acceptance we need—either from God or from other people—will forever escape our grasp.

Most people would be shocked to realize just how much that fear drives them. Workaholics, afraid of losing the recognition and respect they crave, push themselves like slaves to get the job done at any cost. Logging hours of overtime and spending late nights at the office, they strive to make themselves indispensable (and, therefore, unrejectable). People-pleasers, frightened of others' disapproval, sacrifice their own destiny and identity to adapt to what others want. Morphing their personalities to suit one person and then another, they conform to the expectations of co-workers, family members, and church friends. They don a different mask for each group until they lose track of who they really are.

Rebels cope with the fear of rejection by taking a different approach. Convinced they'll never win the acceptance they want, they purposely push people away. They preempt the inevitable by rejecting others before others reject them.

I have some friends whose daughter took that route. A mystery to her parents, she rebelled against them all her life even though they loved her dearly and gave her everything she wanted. I asked her one day why she did it and she said, "Because I didn't *feel* accepted." Her parents are so devoted to her that I had to wonder whether her feelings were real or imagined. Either way, the results were the same. Her fear of rejection devastated her own life and her family's. It inflicted suffering on everyone involved.

Even mature Christians, leaders in the church, are often driven by fear. I've seen evidence of it in ministers' conferences when preachers start asking each other questions like, "How many members does your church have? Have you written any books lately? Have you had many speaking invitations this year?"

Such questions may be innocent. They might be nothing more than one minister expressing interest in another. But many times there's something else going on. Fear-driven people are trying to validate their own value and worth. They're trying to find out by comparing themselves with others if they are superior or inferior, more acceptable or less acceptable than someone else.

The Bible warns us not to do that. It says that people who go around "comparing themselves among themselves, are not wise" (2 Corinthians 10:12). Comparison is the high-octane fuel of fear and shame. Rather than inspiring us to excel as unique individuals, it keeps us in competition mode—always straining to do more than somebody else, to be more than they are, and have more than they do. Comparison brings us under the influence of the spirit of the world and as Christians, we should never be involved in it. When we compare ourselves to someone else and come out on top, we elevate ourselves in pride. If we come out below, we feel degraded. Both results are ungodly, so either way, we lose.

That's why some years ago, Dennis and I decided to avoid all conversations that invite comparison. If we want to express interest in other ministers, we ask them how they are and if there's anything we can do to serve them. We ask about the person, not the product. We make it a point *not* to ask other ministers about the size and growth statistics of their ministries (and we don't answer such questions ourselves) because all too often somebody ends up feeling insignificant.

Granted, they shouldn't feel that way, but they do because they've been influenced by the world's standards of significance. They evaluate their ministries or their lives according to the same criteria the heathens use—wealth, numbers, size, and influence. Afraid that other ministers won't respect them if they find out their church is small, they're tempted to exaggerate the attendance. Scared they'll be considered inconsequential, they add on to the Lord's leadings. If He prompts them to take a single meal to a struggling family, they come up with a "vision" for a soup kitchen to feed hundreds.

In the fear-inspired world of comparison, bigger is always better. But that's not God's world. He doesn't have that perspective. He evaluates our success by asking only one question: Are we doing what He told us to do? Nothing more, nothing less. To Him, the size of our task is irrelevant. The money involved means nothing. The numbers, who cares?

As God sees it, the significance of our efforts is not determined by *what* we're doing but by *Who* told us to do it.

That's why comparison and the devilish fear it engenders are so ridiculous. God has given each one of us a unique assignment. We literally cannot be compared to each other. We are one-of-a-kind individuals with distinctive gifts. First Peter 2:5 refers to us as "lively stones" because no two stones are exactly alike; they're all different shapes, colors, and sizes.

God has always been a fan of stones. In the Old Testament, He commanded that His Temple, as well as all His altars and memorials, be built with them. Never once in the entire Bible, did God instruct anybody to build anything for Him out of brick.

Bricks were man's idea. The tower of Babel bunch came up with it. When they decided to disobey God's command by congregating in once place (instead of going out and filling up the earth), they started their own ungodly building program. "They said to one another, 'Come, let us make bricks and bake them thoroughly.' They had brick for stone, and they had asphalt for mortar" (Genesis 11:3 NKJV).

The worldly-minded Babylonians didn't like what God liked. They didn't delight in the uniqueness and individuality of stones. They wanted building blocks that were all the same. They demanded conformity because they were under the influence of the devil. Conformity, comparison, and competition are high on his agenda. He promotes them because they make people afraid of each other. They give us reasons to reject each other. And they're as wicked as the tower of Babel.

Reconciliation: God's Answer to the Fear of Rejection

Thank God, sometime after my sessions with Ava during my Bible School class on righteousness, I got liberated from the brick-makers mentality and the fear that goes with it. The Lord did for me through His Word what Mr. Duce couldn't. He set me permanently and gloriously free to be...me.

In those days, Proverbs 29:25 became one of my favorite verses: "Fearing people is a dangerous trap, but to trust the LORD means safety."

I like that verse because it doesn't just tell us to get over our fear of what people think. It doesn't scold us for wanting to be accepted. That would be pointless. The need for acceptance is built into our nature. We can't be healthy and whole without it, and God doesn't suggest that we try.

He simply warns us that looking to other people to satisfy that need is dangerous because they'll always disappoint us. It's not necessarily their fault. It's just that nobody is perfect. Even family members and friends who love us can sometimes be insensitive, fickle, or inconsistent. So if we depend on them for affirmation, we're destined for a lifetime of rejection and hurt.

The only one Person we can fully trust to provide the acceptance we need is God. Unlike men, He doesn't turn His back on us when we fall short. He always accepts us and forgives us. He never gives us the cold shoulder—even when we feel like we deserve it—because He has *reconciled* us to Himself once and for all through the blood of Jesus.

Reconciliation is God's answer to the fear of rejection! It transforms us from insecure scaredy cats into bold, beloved sons of God. It reminds us that even when we were at our worst, in active rebellion against God, He accepted us. And it assures us that no sin is big enough to separate us from His love. Romans 5:8,10-11, referring to the liberating truth of reconciliation again and again, says that

> ...*God demonstrated His own love toward us, in that while we were yet sinners, Christ died for us... For if while we were enemies, we were reconciled to God through the death of His Son, much more, having been reconciled, we shall be saved by His life. And not only this, but we also exult in God through our Lord*

Jesus Christ, through whom we have now received the reconciliation.

The first chapter of Colossians, verses 21-22 say it this way:

...although you were formerly alienated and hostile in mind, engaged in evil deeds, yet He has now reconciled you in His fleshly body through death, in order to present you before Him holy and blameless and beyond reproach.

Reconcile is a wonderful word! It means to restore, to put things back the way they were before sin existed, to re-establish relationship, to turn enemies into friends. When God reconciled you to Himself, He made you 100% acceptable in His sight forever. He restored your relationship with Him. He removed your transgressions from Him as far as the east is from the west.[8]

When you have a revelation of reconciliation, you never have to fear man again. You can shrug it off when people reject you. You can smile and say, "Hey, that's no big deal! God is my friend. He thinks I'm wonderful and beyond reproach, why should I worry about what anybody else thinks?"

Once you know that God embraces and accepts you, you can stop living to make other people happy—and that's great because pleasing people is impossible anyway. They're fickle. What makes them happy today may make them unhappy tomorrow. What delights one person offends another. You can never please everyone and, thank God, that's not your job. Your job is to please the Lord. If you understand that, you can just truck on down the road praising Him, doing what He's told you to do, and enjoying life.

[8] Psalm 103:12

That's what Jesus did.

People didn't make it a cakewalk for Him, though. They gave Him all kinds of flak. He encountered such tremendous disapproval that Bible says, "He was despised and rejected and forsaken by men..." (Isaiah 53:3 AMP). Even Jesus' immediate family rejected Him. At the peak of His ministry, they refused to attend His meetings. One time, His mother and brothers actually stood outside one of His services and sent somebody to interrupt His preaching because they wanted to talk to Him.[9] They showed no respect for what He was doing.

The folks in Jesus' hometown of Nazareth acted even worse. When He preached in their synagogue, they got so mad that they tried to throw Him off a cliff. If that wasn't bad enough, the Pharisees hounded Him everywhere He went. They accused Him of being demon-possessed. They called Him a blasphemer and said He worked for the devil.

The multitudes didn't treat Him much better. They were happy enough to accept the free gifts Jesus gave them; they wanted the healing and deliverance He offered; they gladly chowed down on the multiplied loaves and fishes; yet for the most part, they rejected Jesus personally. "He came to His own, and His own did not receive Him."[10] He didn't let it bother Him, though. He never got offended or retaliated against those who mistreated and judged Him. He never even tried to defend Himself. He just continued to love them and do the work of God.

He didn't add-on to that work, either. He didn't push Himself to exhaustion trying to meet everybody's needs. He didn't let people put so many demands on him that they wore

---

[9] Matthew 12:46

[10] John 1:12

Him out and left Him with nothing else to give. (That's what they'll do if you let them. They'll use you up and then throw you away.) Jesus did only what God directed Him to do. He refrained from rushing in to fix every situation. He waited until He heard or saw that somebody had faith to receive. At the pool of Bethesda, for example, He walked past multitudes of sick people and ministered to just one—the paralyzed man who, at Jesus' command, picked up his bed and walked.

"But I thought Jesus cared about everybody!" you might say. He did. But He also understood when He was on earth that He wasn't called to minister to every single person. He wasn't called to work every field, just the ones that were ripe for harvest.

That's something I didn't know when I first began to minister to people. In my early days working at the church in Los Angeles, I almost allowed a drug addict to leave her children at my house while she went away for a while to *get herself together*. Thank goodness, I checked with my pastor about it first. He asked me why I was doing it.

"Because she asked me…and because she needs help," I said.

That's when he taught me about working in ripe harvest fields. He helped me see that the addict wasn't ready to change; she just wanted me to help with her kids so she could be free to do more drugs. "Vikki, you don't run to meet the need every time somebody cries out for help," he said. "People who aren't ready to listen to the Word will just keep on doing the same things that got them in a mess in the first place. Then they'll cry out for help again. Those kinds of people will exhaust you and waste your time. Let the Lord show you who's ripe for ministry. When you work fields that aren't ripe, the fruit will be bitter; when you work the fields that are, the fruit will be sweet."

That was some of the best counsel I've ever gotten. It could have come straight from the lips of Jesus himself because He lived by it throughout His ministry on earth.

How did He manage to do it? How was He able to be impervious to people's driving demands and do only what God led Him to do? What kept Him from caring about their criticism and rejection? What gave Him the guts to say to their faces, "Your approval or disapproval means nothing to me" (John 5:41)?

He knew who He was—the bonafide Son of Almighty God.

He had a revelation of how much God loved and valued Him. He understood that His identity and worth was not determined by other people's opinions of Him but by what God's Word said about Him. Jesus was completely convinced that God accepted and treasured Him; He was completely focused, not on pleasing people, but on pleasing His Father; and as a result, He was completely free.

"But that's Jesus!" you might say. "It's easy for Him to feel valuable. Look at who He is."

It ought to be just as easy for you. Look at the price He paid for you.

The price that someone is willing to pay for something is what determines its value. Dennis and I discovered that the hard way in the early years of our marriage when we butted heads over the purchase of a car. Dennis thought the car was wonderful. I thought it was a waste of money and let him know it in no uncertain terms. We debated the issue for days, but the vote stayed split as Dennis continued to lobby for the purchase and I staunchly opposed it.

Eventually our pastor broke the tie. He kept hammering at me about submitting to my husband and I wearied of his condemnation and gave in. "Okay, Dennis, go ahead and buy the car if you believe God wants us to have it," I said.

Even as we boarded the plane for North Carolina to pick up our purchase, I knew in my heart the car would break down before we got home. It did. We drove as far as Little Rock, Arkansas, and the water pump went out. We spent the night in a hotel while it was being repaired. From then on, things went from bad to worse. It seemed like every time Dennis left town, the car broke down and left me stranded somewhere.

Finally I decided to sell it. I put an ad in the newspaper offering the car for what I considered to be a very fair price considering what we paid for it and how much we spent in repairs. The first person who called said he'd buy the car for $200 less than what I wanted. I said no. The second caller offered me $1,000 less. (This was going the wrong direction.) I said no. Three months later, after spending more money for classified ads and another $300 on car repairs, I decided to sell it to the next person who called—no matter what they offered.

By then, I'd learned my lesson. I understood that the value of the car wasn't determined by what the Kelley Blue Book said it was worth. It wasn't determined by what I wanted for it. The value was determined by what someone was willing to pay.

Value=Price Paid. That's not just true when it comes to automobiles. It's true about me and you. Our value has been determined by the price God paid for us. Our worth was forever established when God purchased us with the life of His only begotten Son.

Staggering as seems, *Value=Price Paid* means that to God, we are as precious as Jesus. It means that He loves us, as the redeemed, just as much as He loves the Redeemer. Jesus confirmed it. When He prayed for us just before He went to the cross, He said to the Father, "You have sent Me, and have loved them as You have loved Me" (John 17:23).

Others can think what they want. Their approval or disapproval of you doesn't affect your worth. It's been set for time and eternity by the Creator of the Universe and it can't be changed.

He paid the highest price ever paid...for you.

What You Don't Know CAN Hurt You

The Bible leaves no doubt about it: God has done everything necessary to free us from fear forever. He has loved us perfectly. "There is no fear in love; but perfect love casts out fear" (1 John 4:18). He has conquered the devil who is the author of all fear and put him under our feet. He has given us the right to boldly say, "The LORD is my helper; I will not fear..." (Hebrews 13:6).

Why then do countless believers still put up with it? Why do they remain imprisoned by fears of every kind?

The answer is simple. It's because the devil has sold them a lie. He's done to Christians all over this planet what the Japanese army did to U.S. General Jonathan Wainwright.

During World War II, General Wainwright was a prisoner of war in a remote POW camp in Manchuria. Incarcerated in May of 1942 when his troops were so decimated by casualties, hunger, and disease that he was forced to surrender, Wainwright spent the rest of the war guarded by the Japanese as a trophy—the only American general they'd ever captured. He suffered greatly during that time, not only from the abuse of the enemy but from the crushing shame of having waved the white flag. He deteriorated both in body and soul becoming, at least in his own eyes, little more than a crippled failure leaning on a cane.

His only hope was that the Allies would win the war. Which, of course, they did.

But on August 15, 1945, when Japan surrendered, nobody told General Wainwright.

His captors kept him ignorant of what had happened. So for a few terrible weeks, everything at the camp in Manchuria stayed the same. Malnourished, dysentery-plagued prisoners remained in their cells. Well-fed, fully-armed Japanese soldiers swaggered and bullied just as they had for the previous three years, all the while knowing that the power they wielded was based on a lie.

No doubt, beneath their braggadocio their hearts pounded with fear knowing that eventually General Wainwright would find out they'd been defeated. He'd get word of the Allied victory and turn the tables on them. As an officer on the winning side, he had the right to strip his enemies of their weapons and take charge of the camp. He had the authority to turn his captors into captives.

And with the power of United States military backing him, he could do it in a heartbeat.

That's exactly the situation the devil is in these days. Did you know that? He and his forces have already been defeated. Jesus has conquered them through the cross and resurrection, "Having disarmed principalities and powers, He made a public spectacle of them, triumphing over them in it" (Colossians 2:15). Jesus has done everything necessary to "render powerless him who had the power of death, that is, the devil; and...deliver those who through fear of death were subject to slavery all their lives" (Hebrews 2:14-15 NRSV).

As born-again believers, we're no longer POW's and the devil knows it. He is shaking in his boots because he understands that we don't have to be afraid of anything anymore—including him—because "we are more than conquerors through Him who loved us" (Romans 8:37).

"I don't know about that," somebody might say, "the devil still has some authority."

Not according to Jesus, he doesn't.

Jesus said, "All authority is given unto me in heaven and in earth" (Matthew 28:18 NKJV). *All authority!* That means there's none left over for the devil. Jesus possesses every bit of it and He has delegated it to us as His representatives.

At the end of WW II, General MacArthur expelled the enemy troops from every island in the Pacific, achieved absolute victory, and gave officers like General Jonathan Wainwright the authority to liberate every POW camp in Asia. Jesus has done essentially the same thing for us. He's achieved absolute victory over Satan and said to us:

Behold, I give you the authority to trample on serpents and scorpions, and over all the power of the enemy, and nothing shall by any means hurt you.

Luke 10:19

Authority is a marvelous thing! The dictionary defines it as "the right to command and enforce obedience; lawful permission to execute power; ability to bring judgment or justice." According to that definition, as Christians, we have the right to command the kingdom of darkness to obey us. We have legal permission to execute power over the devil and all His works. We have the power to spiritually enforce the will and Word of God so that His justice is done on earth as it is in heaven.

Exousia, which is the Greek word translated "authority" in Luke 10:19, refers specifically to delegated authority. It's the kind of authority that police officers are given by the city. To get a sense of how it works, think about how a policeman directs traffic. He stands in the middle of the street, raises his hand, and vehicles weighing 2,000 pounds or more come to a halt. Obviously the policeman can't physically force the vehicles to stop, yet they do so anyway because the drivers know the officer has authority. He is backed by the power of the city. If they ignore him, they'll find themselves in heavy duty trouble.

The devil understands the same thing about you. He knows that as God's child you've been given His delegated authority and you represent all of heaven's power. When you speak God's Word, God himself backs you up. When you declare God's commands, it's as though He is declaring those commands Himself.

If that system sounds familiar to you, it should. As we saw in Genesis, that's the kind of dominion Adam and Eve exercised in the Garden. They operated in God's delegated authority. When they spoke, creation obeyed them just as if God was speaking. Although the devil robbed mankind of that authority through the fall, Jesus legally reclaimed it through the cross and the resurrection. Then, being the true Giver that He is, He gave the authority back to His disciples. He said:

> *"All authority has been given to Me in heaven and on earth. Go therefore and make disciples of all the nations, baptizing them in the name of the Father and*

the Son and the Holy Spirit, teaching them to observe all that I commanded you; and lo, I am with you always, even to the end of the age."

Matthew 18:18-20 NASB

The ministry of Jesus hasn't ended; He has delegated it to us. We are His Body on the earth now. We have both the authority and the responsibility to carry on what He began. His mission is now our mission: that men may have life, and that they may have it more abundantly (John 10:10).

Why should we, as Christians, keep sitting around waiting for God to do something? God has put the proverbial ball in our court. He is waiting on us! He's expecting us to act on the instructions Jesus gave us when He said, "You go do the works you've seen Me do and even greater. You cast out demons. You lay hands on the sick and they'll recover. You resist the devil and he'll flee from you."

"Well, God is in control," somebody might say. "I like to leave things to Him."

He didn't give us that option. He made us co-laborers "and joint heirs with Christ" (Romans 8:17). He raised us up together, and made us sit together in the heavenly places in Him:

...far above all principality and power and might and dominion, and every name that is named, not only in this age but also in that which is to come. And He put all things under His feet, and gave Him to be head over all things to the church, which is His body, the fullness of Him who fills all in all.

Ephesians 1:21-23

Jesus is the head, we are the body. Although the body can't do anything without the head, the reverse is also true.

The head can't get anything done without the body. If you're sitting in your living room and you get thirsty, can your head go into the kitchen all by itself and get a drink of water? Of course not! It needs the cooperation of your body.

By the same token, when Jesus wants something done on the earth, He needs our cooperation. (It's stunning, I know, but that's the way He set things up.) Just as surely as we depend on Him to provide us with the wisdom and power to do His will, He depends on us to exercise His delegated authority and put His will into action.

Before my mother went to heaven, she signed a Power of Attorney so that I could act on her behalf when she was unable to do so for herself. For three years, I exercised that power to write checks from her bank account and pay her bills. I called her insurance company and spoke to them as if her policy was mine. I worked with the hospital to accept or refuse treatments for her. I spoke and acted in all kinds of situations as her legal representative.

When Jesus went to heaven, He gave us His Power of Attorney. He commanded us to use it to carry out His will. He commissioned us to speak and act on His behalf. He said to us, as the Church, "...I will give you the keys of the kingdom of heaven, and whatever you bind on earth will be bound in heaven, and whatever you loose on earth will be loosed in heaven" (Matthew 16:19 NKJV). The Phillips Translation reads this way: "I will give you the keys of the kingdom of Heaven; whatever you forbid on earth will be what is forbidden in heaven and whatever you permit on earth will be what is permitted in Heaven."

That doesn't sound to me like Jesus was telling us that we could relax and just let God be responsible for everything. It sounds like He was delegating responsibility to us.

The Miracle I Could Have Missed

Believers who shy away from that authority don't understand how much difference it can make. They don't realize it can literally save lives. But it can. I found that one night years ago when the phone rang and I got news nobody wants to hear. Someone dear to me, an unsaved relative of mine, had disappeared from his home, carrying a gun with the intent to kill. Initially, he'd planned to murder his wife who got fed up with his alcoholism and abuse, packed up, and left him. When he couldn't find her, he called my mother to say he was turning the gun on himself.

After begging him not to do it, Mother called me in a panic. We both knew his suicide threat was real. Years of hopelessness and rage had so frayed his ability to cope with life that he'd totally lost his grip. Alone and without God, he was more than ready to pull the trigger.

This particular relative didn't like me at all—and hadn't for a long time. As far as he was concerned, I could go to hell and he wouldn't care. But I didn't feel the same way. It didn't matter to me that he wouldn't speak to me when we visited on holidays. It didn't matter that he told me to my face that he hated me. He was family. I loved him and was not willing to let the devil have him.

That's why I'd been praying for him for so many years. Acts 16:31 says, "Believe in the Lord Jesus, and you shall be saved, you and your household." Based on that promise, I'd claimed the salvation of this relative and I wasn't about to give up on it. So instead of crying and wringing my hands in fear, I hung up the phone and exercised my authority.

Together, Dennis and I prayed and then spoke to the spirit of suicide that was tormenting my relative. In Jesus' Name, we forbade it to take his life.

After we prayed, I called the police department in the city where he lived and gave them his license plate number. They issued an all points bulletin, found him, and locked him up for 48 hours. It didn't do much good, though. When he got out of jail, he repeated the scenario two more times.

The third time my mother called, hysterical, to tell me he was trapped in a phone booth with his gun trained on the police surrounding him. His plan this time was to threaten them with his weapon until they killed him. Good plan. It would have worked, I'm sure, if it hadn't been for one thing: Dennis and I kept using our spiritual authority. We continued to forbid the spirit of suicide to take my relative's life.

I don't mind telling you, I had plenty of opportunity to be frightened by the situation. An entire SWAT team had guns pointed at somebody I love. They were ready to kill him—and for good reason! But I refused to give fear any foothold. I chose to trust God and act on Philippians 1:28 which says:

And do not [for a moment] be frightened or intimidated in anything by your opponents and adversaries, for such [constancy and fearlessness] will be a clear sign (proof and seal) to them of [their impending] destruction, but [a sure token and evidence] of your deliverance and salvation, and that from God.

When I asked the Lord for further guidance about how to take charge of the situation, I heard Him say to me: *Make him hungry for what you have.*

How am I supposed to do that? I wondered. *He won't even speak to me. He hates even being around me because the light in my life makes the darkness in his seem even darker.* Figuring the only thing I could do was pray for him, I said, "Lord, You cause him to hunger and thirst for what he sees in me."

A few days later I got the shock of my life. My suicidal relative—alive and without gunshot wounds but as gruff as ever—called me on the phone. Although he hadn't spoken to me in years, he didn't even bother to say hello. He just blurted out what was on his mind.

"Do you want to know why I hate you?" he said.

"Yes, I've been wondering that for a long time," I answered.

"I hate you because you have so much peace."

Knowing an open door when I see one, I walked through with boldness. "You can have the same peace I have if you'll give your life to Jesus."

He ended the conversation by asking if he could come and stay with me for a while. I agreed and sent him a plane ticket. He didn't act very happy to see me when we met at the airport. I don't think he really wanted to be there but the Spirit of God had compelled him. Not long after he visited me, he was born again and filled with the Holy Spirit.

Looking back, it's clear that his survival and salvation are nothing short of a miracle. But this is also clear. If Dennis and I had just shrugged our shoulders and left everything up to God that miracle wouldn't have happened. If we had remained POWs of fear, my relative would have died as the devil's captive.

But thank God, he didn't.

Thank God, Dennis and I had heard the good news that through Jesus our enemy has been defeated and the victory has been won. We knew we had heaven backing us, so we exercised our authority, turned the tables on the devil, and in the Name of the Lord, we took charge of the camp.

CHAPTER 11

Never Let Go

*Therefore, do not throw away your confidence, which
has a great reward. For you have need of endurance,
so that when you have done the will of God, you may
receive what was promised.*

Hebrews 10:35-36 NASB

If Duke had been a Christian, he would have lived the abundant life. I'm sure of it. Given the chance, he would have gotten a firm grip on the Gospel, fought the good fight of faith literally tooth and toenail, and hung in there until he walked away a winner.

Yep, Duke would have made one devil-dominating, doubt-conquering disciple.

Except for one thing.

He was a Doberman pinscher.

Being a dog, he couldn't get saved, of course. (I'm aware of that, I assure you.) But even so, he's inspired me often over the years as I've battled my way out of the bondages of shame, blame, guilt, and fear. If I ever got weary in well doing, if I was ever tempted to throw myself a pity party and give up, all I had to do was remember Duke: brown eyes narrowed and ablaze with determination, muscles flexed and straining, jaw locked and teeth bared around a saliva-drenched strand of rope.

To Duke, tug-of-war was no game. It was serious business. Dennis and I found that out the first time we grabbed hold of his rope and tried to wrestle it away from him. We were newlyweds back then with no children, so Duke was our entertainment. We enjoyed who-knows-how-many hours of fun employing all manner of force and trickery to pry him loose from his prize.

We started out, as most dog-owners do, with the straight-forward strategy of ganging up on him—Dennis and me on one side of the rope, Duke pulling against us on the other. Together we outmanned and outweighed him, but it made no difference. It was his rope; he knew it; and we weren't getting it. Toenails dug into the lawn, teeth imbedded in twine, he refused to let it go.

Once we tired of that approach, we became less sportsman-like. Leaving Dennis to tug against Duke, I would ambush the dog from behind, seize his jaws, and try to wedge them open just enough for Dennis to yank the rope free. It never worked, though. Duke just wagged his stumpy tail and relished making fools of us. Apart from that, nothing changed. Duke's jowls remained set, smiling, and in firm possession of the rope.

When the ambush had clearly failed, I resorted to my final and most forceful attack. I latched onto the rope and swung it in circles with Duke still clamped to the other end. Spinning round and round, faster and faster, Duke's massive paws would eventually lift off the ground and he'd go airborne, orbiting me like a 60-pound black and brown satellite. But it didn't matter. He still hung on, eyes glinting with defiance, regardless of how long or fast he flew. He never once let go of the rope.

Recently when I was chatting with Ava on the phone and she told me how she wished more believers would fight their way through to freedom like I have, I thought again about Duke. I flashed back on his fierce commitment to winning the war of the rope. That kind of commitment, I realized, was what had made the difference for me.

Sitting in my bedroom chair all those years ago, imprisoned by despair, I'd caught hold of a rope that could pull me to freedom. I got a revelation that a life of liberty could be mine. I heard Jesus say:

Come into fellowship with me if you are tired and burdened and I will refresh and release you. Take the burden of responsibility I give you and thereby discover your life and your destiny. I am gentle and humble; I am willing to relate to you and to permit you to learn at your own rate; then, in fellowship with me, you will discover the meaning of life. My fellowship will release you, and my companionship will direct you on your journey.

Matthew 11:28-30 BCJ

A life without add-ons. A life of rest and refreshing like I'd never known before. A life of destiny and meaning, fellowshipping with God as a human being dearly loved by Him rather than a human doing always trying to prove myself worthy. That's what I glimpsed in the months after my meltdown.

And, grabbing it with the determination of a Doberman, I refused to let go.

Some people think of Christianity as something sweet. They think of it as all soft and fluffy and nice. But that's not the way it is when we're in a tug-of-war against the devil who's trying to rob us of the blessings of redemption. We can't afford to be soft and sweet when we're battling for our blood-bought freedom and taking our stand against the Serpent who engineered the fall.

To win that fight, we must be like Duke. Ember-eyed, lock-jawed, and immovable. We must know what's ours, latch onto it with unrelenting resolve, and refuse to let go.

"That's Mine and I Know It!"

Knowing what's ours in Christ begins—but doesn't end—with finding out exactly what the blessings of redemption are. The Bible is full of them. We'll spend the rest of our lives discovering and understanding them all. But in the end, it will all come back to this: Through Jesus, God reclaimed for us what Adam and Eve lost in the Garden.

- He made us righteous with His own righteousness.

- He reconciled us to Himself and gave us back our relationship with Him.

- He restored our significance, our value, and our dominion.

- He delivered us from the curse: from the spiritual bondage of sin, spiritual death, and alienation from God; from emotional bondages such as fear, shame, guilt, depression, and loneliness; and from the physical bondage of things like sickness and poverty.

- He bestowed on us His *blessing* which, according the Biblical definition of the word *empowers us to succeed*

228

and prosper in every endeavor and triumph continuously in every area of life.

Maybe you're already familiar with those truths. Maybe you've read scriptures, heard sermons, and read stacks of books about what belongs to you through Jesus. If so, that's great because knowing what the Bible says is where the journey begins. But head knowledge alone isn't enough. A mere mental understanding of Scripture won't change your life.

Dennis and I have a friend in ministry who proved that in a striking way. He went to seminary as a young man; learned enough of the Bible to pass all his exams, graduate, and become a licensed minister. He served as the pastor of a church for 20 years—before he was ever born again. Think of it. All that time, he knew what God's Word said but it didn't change him. It didn't make any real difference in his life. He knew the facts of the Gospel with his brain, but he didn't let the revelation get down in his heart where it could save him and empower him to practice what he preached.

Shocking, isn't it?

Yet we've all done it. We may not have missed out on being born again like he did, but we've still made the same basic mistake. We've learned Scriptural truths with our intellect; we've heard sermons in church; we've chirped, "Yes, amen! Amen!" and then gone home to leave our Bibles unopened and our behavior unchanged. We've given lip service to revelations that never showed up in our lives.

I've already admitted that's what I did in my first 25 years as a Christian. I settled for a mental understanding of the riches of redemption. I didn't spend enough time in the Word for it to travel from my head to my heart. And that failed journey of inches cost me dearly.

That's why I'm so doggedly determined now to encourage you to do what I didn't back then: *Finish the process.* Build the revelation of what belongs to you as a believer into the depths of your soul. Become convinced with every fiber of your being that the liberty Jesus paid for belongs to you. Be able to say with absolute conviction, "That's mine. I know it. And I'm going to have it in my life."

When my daughter was younger, she and I used to watch the movie *Anne of Green Gables* every few months. One of our favorite moments was when Anne's best friend begged her to keep a secret and Anne declared, "Wild horses cannot take it from me!" That's the attitude you need to have toward the blessings of redemption. You must be so sure they're yours—not just your neighbor's, not just your pastor's, but yours—that wild horses couldn't drag them away from you.

I developed that kind of confidence in my own life by identifying individual blessings and going after them one by one. When I decided to get free of perfectionism, I specifically targeted that freedom and built my faith for it. I developed an inner image of how it would change my life so that I knew exactly what I was aiming for. I followed the instructions in Colossians 3:1 that says:

> *Since you have been raised to new life with Christ, set your sights on the realities of heaven, where Christ sits at God's right hand in the place of honor and power.*

I'm not saying that I set my sights on the future I will have after I die, when I actually go to heaven. That's not what the verse means. It means set your sights on the things that heaven has for you rather than your earthly circumstances; fix your eyes not on the problem but on the Solution. When I set my sights on heaven's realities, I stopped thinking about how insecure and unacceptable I felt; I focused instead on how perfect and righteous Jesus has made me. I put my attention on the peace, favor, and freedom that's mine in Him.

In other words, I took what God's Word says about me and made it my bull's eye.

Most Christians don't even have a target, much less a bull's eye. They're like Charlie Brown in the Peanuts comic strip I saw a few years ago. The first frame showed Charlie practicing archery. His equipment included not only a bow and arrow but a bucket of paint and a brush. Subsequent frames showed him shooting arrows at random and then painting targets around them. Explaining his tactics to an indignant and mystified Lucy, he said, "This way I never miss!"

It's silly, I know, but I see believers living that way every day. They float through life and wherever they end up they say, "Well, I guess this is God's will for me." Truth be told, however, they don't have a clue what God's will is. They're just taking whatever life throws at them. They're just trying to survive.

What a tragedy! God wants more than that for His children. He wants us to live a life of satisfaction and fulfillment. He has a purpose and a plan for each one of us, a unique assignment that only we can fulfill.

"But Vikki, I don't know exactly what God's plan for me is."

Start with what's in the Bible. Most of what you need to know is written there in black and white. So get it squarely in your sights. Begin to see yourself living free; see yourself living in God's promises and being who He says you are. It's not good enough just to want those things. On the inside, you must see yourself possessing them.

That's what the apostle Paul did. He said, "We don't look at the troubles we can see now; rather, we fix our gaze on things that cannot be seen. For the things we see now are temporal and subject to change, but the things we cannot see will last forever" (2 Corinthians 4:18). The idea of looking at things you can't see sounds like an oxymoron (especially when what you *can* see is screaming in your face), but it can be done.

How?

By meditating on God's Word.

Meditating includes more than just reading. It involves taking the Word into yourself in a way that makes it a part of you. The Hebrew word translated *meditate* in the Bible has three distinct connotations. The first one is to mutter. All of us know how to mutter. We do it without even thinking about it. We talk to ourselves when we're in our kitchen about the things we need from the grocery store. We mutter about the other drivers who annoy us when we're in the car. Back when I got serious about my deliverance, I replaced that kind of muttering with meditation of God's Word. Over the years, it's become a habit for me. Whether I'm having my devotional time, caught in a traffic jam, or trotting along on the treadmill, I'm constantly yapping away, speaking the Word over whatever area of my life I'm targeting at the time.

The second connotation of meditation is to ponder. When we ponder the Word, we think about how it applies to our life. We ask ourselves questions like *What would my life look like if I was totally free of insecurity and shame? How would my relationships be different if fear had absolutely no grip on me?* Then we visualize and contemplate the answer.

The third connotation is my favorite and it's this: to chew like a cow chews its cud. Most of us, whether or not we've spent time on a farm, are familiar with this process. A cow eats a mouthful of grass, chews it once, and swallows. Then it regurgitates and repeats the process until the grass is so refined that all the nutrients are released and become a part of the cow.

I know this doesn't sound very ladylike but when it comes to God's Word, I'm always chewing the cud. Spiritually, I am absolutely bovine and make no apologies for it. When I'm in the shower in the morning, or making coffee, or doing the dishes I don't just let my mind wander around grazing on any thought it finds; I put it to work on whatever promise the Lord is quickening to me that day. If I'm facing an adverse situation such as sickness or lack, I chew on scriptures that address the issue. When my mind must busy itself with other things, I swallow those verses. Later, I bring them back up and start chewing again.

Chew, swallow, chew, swallow. Meditate, mutter, ponder. As you do that, you'll eventually absorb the Word so completely that it becomes part of who you are. It influences your mind, will, and emotions. It creates images within you so that you can visualize the Word coming to pass in your life and see the unseen.

"Are you suggesting I should use my imagination when I read the Bible?" somebody might ask.

I certainly am. Our imagination is one of the most powerful tools that God has given us. He expects us to use it. He wants us to feed it with heavenly things, to activate it with His Word so that we can soar above our present circumstances and see His limitless possibilities for our life. Whatever we can see with our imagination we can have. God said so Himself. In Genesis 11:6, He said, "...nothing will be restrained from them, which they have imagined to do."

Your imagination, fueled by the Word, can radically alter your destiny. I'm walking proof of it. Nobody who grew up the way I did should be able to have the kind of joy-filled freedom I enjoy today. When I was young, I didn't even know anyone who lived like this. I couldn't have imagined it. But meditating on God's Word changed that. It enabled me to introduce new tidbits of freedom into my imagination and see a new outcome for myself. It empowered me to dream new dreams. And now those dreams are my reality.

The life I have today isn't something I stumbled into by accident. By the grace of God and the power of the Holy Spirit, I've been able to build it line by line, precept by precept, because I caught hold of verses like these:

> *My son, attend to my words; incline thine ear unto my sayings. Let them not depart from thine eyes; keep them in the midst of thine heart. For they are life unto those that find them, and health to all their flesh (Proverbs 4:20-23).*

> *And be not conformed to this world: but be ye transformed by the renewing of your mind, that ye may prove what is that good, and acceptable, and perfect, will of God (Romans 12:2).*

> *For my thoughts are not your thoughts, neither are your ways my ways, saith the LORD. For as the heavens are higher than the earth, so are my ways higher than your ways, and my thoughts than your thoughts" (Isaiah 55:8-9).*

Without God's thoughts, I would have to spend my life in the lowlands, limited by my own pitiful thinking. But because I have a Bible, I can fly like an eagle. I can open God's Word any time I want and find out what He's thinking. I can renew my mind to what He has said and lift my thoughts to a whole new level. I can learn how to think like God and rise up to receive His blessings.

God's thoughts have already made my life better than I ever expected. And because every day I keep learning more about them, the best is yet to come.

A Voice Activated System

Before we leave him behind, there's one last point I'd like to make about Duke and what I learned from his example: His mouth was his most effective weapon. He took possession of what belonged to him by getting it in his mouth and keeping it there. No matter what happened, he kept his lips wrapped around his rope.

As believers, we essentially do the same thing with the blessings of redemption. We take possession of them with our mouth. We take hold of our redemptive rights by keeping God's Word on our lips, by speaking it continually, by saying out loud—day after day—what the Bible says about us, our family, our circumstances, and our world.

Why is that necessary?

Because God's supernatural power is *voice-activated*. Without our voices speaking in agreement with what God has already promised, there can be no lasting change in our lives. Our voices either open the way or get in the way— depending on how we use them. Our words either advance the plan of God in our lives or hinder it.

When we speak words of faith that agree with the Bible, the Holy Spirit can go to work and bring those words to pass. He can make them real in our life and circumstances. We can see how He does it in the first three verses of the Bible. They tell us that:

In the beginning God created the heaven and the earth. And the earth was without form, and void; and darkness was upon the face of the deep. And the Spirit of God moved upon the face of the waters. And God said, Let there be light: and there was light.

Genesis 1:1-3

Notice that even when the Holy Spirit was present, hovering over the earth in all His power, nothing happened until God spoke. Everything stayed dark until God said the words, "Light be!" That's when the Holy Spirit released His power and darkness fled.

The voice-activated process didn't stop there, either. God kept on speaking. According to Genesis 1, He created everything with His word. He said, "Let there be a firmament. Let there be grass...Let the waters bring forth moving creatures..." That's what God does. It's how He gets things done. He releases His Word, "declaring the end from the beginning."[11] That's His M.O.

Hebrews 11:3 confirms it. It says that God "framed" the worlds with His Word, "so that things which are seen were not made of things which do appear." *Framed* is an interesting word. We usually think of it in terms of building a house, of forming a structure with wood and nails. But, according to the dictionary, *frame* also means to put into words, utter, conceive and create. By that definition, Hebrews 11:3 could read this way: *Through faith we understand that the worlds were put into words; they were uttered, conceived and created by the word of God.*

If God framed the worlds with His Word and we're supposed to follow His example, then we should operate that way too. We should say about ourselves what God says about us.

---

[11] Isaiah 46:10

"But I'm just not comfortable saying those kinds of things," you might say. "It feels awkward."

I know. I felt the same way at first. But I did it anyway and I'm so glad. What a loss it would have been if I'd refused to obey the Lord and say *I love my mother* all those years ago. Talk about uncomfortable! I could hardly bring myself to utter the words at first. They sounded to me like fingernails on a chalkboard because they didn't line up with my feelings or my circumstances. But I said them anyway. I dared to act like God, who "calls those things which do not exist as though they did,"[12] and my relationship with my mother was revolutionized.

Granted, the revolution didn't take place overnight. I didn't just speak God's Word once or twice and see immediate results. I stuck with it. I kept saying it, and saying it, and saying it. Eventually, the Holy Spirit finished the work, and my love for my mother became a reality to me.

Some Christians worry that God's Word won't work that way for them. They're afraid they'll speak the Word in faith and it won't come to pass. But that's impossible. Jesus said, "...assuredly, I say to you, whoever says to this mountain, 'Be removed and be cast into the sea,' and does not doubt in his heart, but believes that those things he says will be done, he will have whatever he says" (Mark 11:23 NKJV).

Faith-filled words activate spiritual laws that are as dependable as the natural law of gravity. Have you ever fallen off a ladder and floated up? Has such a thing ever crossed your mind? No, because you know that gravity never fails.

---

[12] Romans 4:17

God's Word never fails either! In Isaiah 55:10-11 He guarantees us that:

> *... as the rain cometh down, and the snow from heaven, and returneth not thither, but watereth the earth, and maketh it bring forth and bud, that it may give seed to the sower, and bread to the eater: So shall my word be that goeth forth out of my mouth: it shall not return unto me void, but it shall accomplish that which I please, and it shall prosper in the thing whereto I sent it.*

If you think you've put the law of faith-filled words into operation in the past and it didn't work, think again. God's laws always work. Every time. So if you don't get the results you expect, ask Him to show you where you missed it. More often than not, you'll find out you were just in too much of a hurry. That's an easy mistake to make because we've been trained by high speed Internet and fast food restaurants to expect everything now. We want to drive up to the first window, confess the Word, then drive to the second window and pick up what we want. But that's not the way God operates. His system involves waiting. It requires us to "imitate those who through faith and patience inherit the promises" (Hebrews 6:12).

As much as we all want to see quick results in our lives, we must remember that time is not the issue. Victory is the issue. The devil will detour and discourage us if he can get our eyes off the Word and onto the calendar. But if we're willing to stand forever—Doberman-like, with God's promise between our teeth and our toenails dug into the ground—victory will be ours.

Are You a Grasshopper or a Giant?

I must warn you, however, the devil will use unsportsmanlike tactics against you. He'll ambush your thoughts and pressure you with lies to trick you into letting go of what's yours. He'll try to twist your thinking so that you'll stop agreeing with God and start agreeing with him.

If you let him, the devil will get you so focused on the problems in your life and the failures in your past that you'll stop seeing yourself as a dearly-beloved, fully-accepted, holy and righteous child of God, and start seeing yourself once again as an unworthy, sinful worm. He'll convince you that you're a grasshopper instead of a giant. That's what he did to the children of Israel and it robbed them of their Promised Land.

You've probably read the story. When Moses was preparing to lead the Israelites into Canaan, he sent 12 men to spy out the land beforehand. They came back with both good news and bad news. The good news was that the land was rich—flowing with milk and honey, and stocked with grapes as big as basketballs. It was the place of their dreams. The bad news was: "There we saw the giants, the sons of Anak, which come of the giants: and we were in our own sight as grasshoppers, and so we were in their sight" (Numbers 13:33).

Notice, the spies reported as fact that the giants saw them as grasshoppers. But was it really a fact? If so, how did the spies know it? Do you suppose they walked up to one of them and said, "Excuse me, Mr. Giant? What do I look like to you?"

Of course they didn't. The spies had no objective information about how the giants saw them. They made up that part of their report. Because they saw themselves as insignificant, inadequate grasshoppers, they just assumed the Canaanites saw them that way too.

It was the Israelites' thinking—not God's will—that determined their destiny. God had already promised to give them the land. He'd promised to help them defeat its inhabitants—giants or not. The children of Israel had a God-given right to dwell in the Promised Land. But they were robbed of that right by their own thoughts. The devil convinced them they were small and powerless so that's what they became. As a result, they ended up wandering for 40 years, and eventually dying, in the wilderness.

The only two members of the group who didn't die there were Joshua and Caleb. Their outcome was different because they thought differently. They didn't deny the natural realities. They acknowledged that there were some gargantuan dudes in the Promised Land, but it didn't scare them. They didn't react to the giants by seeing themselves as grasshoppers. They focused instead on their God and His Word.

Joshua and Caleb saw themselves as giant-slayers because that's what God said about them. They refused to agree with the lying thoughts of the devil. They ended up enjoying their Promised Land because they agreed with God and said, "Let us go up at once, and possess it; for we are well able to overcome…" (Verse 30).

Our thoughts are a big deal! They will either propel us toward God's promise, or rob us of it. They will either make us, or break us. Unbelieving thoughts deprive us of our divine destiny. That's why we must be vigilant; and when we catch ourselves thinking contrary to the Word, we must go on the attack:

> …*pulling down strongholds, casting down arguments (or imaginations) and every high thing that exalts itself*

*against the knowledge of God, bringing every thought
into captivity to the obedience of Christ.*

2 Corinthians 10:4-5

The word translated *stronghold* in that verse refers to a
mental fortress, an argument or reasoning used to fortify an
opinion and defend it against an opponent. The devil builds
strongholds in our minds by presenting us with thoughts
like, *The Word may work for others, but not for me,* or *This
problem is too big. It's a giant, and I'm a grasshopper. Even
God can't help me now.* There's only one Scriptural way to
deal with such thoughts: bring them into captivity. When
they come to steal God's promises of peace, health, joy, and
prosperity, treat them like the thieves they are.

How do you do that?

First: Identify them. Compare them with John 10:10. It
says, "the thief comes only to steal, and to kill, and to destroy,"
but Jesus has come they we "might have life and might
have it abundantly." Any thought that steals your faith in
God's Word, destroys your God-given hope, or deprives you
of abundant life, comes from the enemy. Any thought that
builds faith, inspires godly expectation, and makes you more
alive is from God.

Second: Whenever you identify a thieving thought,
arrest it and take it into custody. Say right out loud, "Wrong
thought, you have no right in my mind. My body is the temple
of the Holy Spirit so you are trespassing on God's property. I
command you to cease your actions against me and I render
you powerless from this moment forward!"

Third: Pronounce judgment. In our earthly court systems,
after a thief has been arrested, a legal ruling is decreed in his
case. Follow the same protocol spiritually; use the authority
Jesus has given you to bind things in His name, and boldly

declare that the devil no longer has a right to your mind. Job 22:28 says, "You will...decree a thing, and it will be established for you; and light will shine on your ways" (NASB). So decree that your days of distorted thinking are over.

Finally: Sentence the thief. Take the thoughts that have stolen God's promises from you and sentence them to a rehabilitation program. To *rehabilitate* means to restore, renovate, return to normalcy, refurbish, make whole again, reconstruct, rebuild, and recondition. You can rehabilitate any wayward thought—no matter how incorrigible—by locking it up in God's Word and keeping it there until it's transformed.

If you catch a thought thief in your mind telling you that you're a failure, take it to the Word. Spend time meditating on the scriptures that say you're more than a conqueror through Him who loves you; that you're the head and not the tail, above only and not beneath; that you can do all things through Christ who strengthens you; and that Christ always leads you in triumph.

Write those verses on index cards and tape them to your refrigerator, your car dashboard, your bathroom mirror, and your computer screen. Mutter them while you're getting dressed in the morning. Make up tunes and sing them on your way to work. Ponder them on your coffee break. Chew on them as you drift off to sleep at night.

"But what if I still feel like a failure?"

When your thoughts are in the process of rehabilitation it doesn't matter how you feel. Would it make any difference if you woke up in the morning and didn't feel married? Not if you have a legal document that proves you are, it wouldn't! The truth is the truth regardless of our emotions. So if the devil starts badgering you with negative feelings, get out your legal document—your Bible—and show him what it says. Rub his nose in reality and remind yourself of the truth.

Don't be timid about it, either. When it comes to dealing with the devil, get aggressive. Go after the strongholds he's built in your mind and absolutely demolish them with the Word. Be like King David was. He didn't mess around with his enemies. He didn't settle for partial victory over them. When he went after Goliath, he whopped him in the forehead with a stone, severed his head from his shoulders, and then routed the entire Philistine army.

In Psalm 18, David summed up his dealings with enemy armies this way:

> *I shattered them, so that they were not able to rise; They fell under my feet. For Thou hast girded me with strength for battle; Thou hast subdued under me those who rose up against me. Thou hast also made my enemies turn their backs to me, And I destroyed those who hated me. They cried for help, but there was none to save, Even to the LORD, but He did not answer them. Then I beat them fine as the dust before the wind; I emptied them out as the mire of the streets.*
>
> Psalm 18:38-42

Too many Christians fight the devil halfway. They push back his thieving thoughts just enough to relieve the immediate pressure. Instead of destroying those thoughts completely, they end up facing them again another day. David didn't make that mistake. Confident that God had equipped him to subdue his enemies, he chased them down and annihilated them. He beat them as fine as dust and then threw the dust in the gutter.

Goliath didn't live to fight another day. David finished the job the first time.

When it comes to dealing with the devil's lies, we need to be like David.

Where the Greatest Victories Are Won

I made a commitment when I started this book to be completely honest; and it would be less than honest to say that the process of fighting your way to freedom is easy. It's not. It's not quick, either. Or pretty. At least, it wasn't for me.

Maybe I had more to deal with than you do. I hope so. But if you're in a similar situation, I want you to know that the first year of my battle was rugged. I didn't spring from my bedroom chair and dance my way to liberty the first day the Lord spoke to me from Matthew 11:28-30. I had to start by slogging through swamps of grief and anger. I had to deal with the searing sense of loss that swept over me as I realized how many years I'd wasted living in bondage, unaware that Jesus had already set me free.

Some days my progress seemed excruciatingly slow. Judging by my former standards of external performance, it looked like I was making no headway at all. Friends and associates accustomed to my infamous production levels asked with puzzled concern, "Vikki, what are you *doing* these days?" I knew they wouldn't understand if I told the truth. If I said, "I'm focusing more right now on *being* than doing," they would have turned away as perplexed as ever.

To encourage myself, I often reminded myself of a letter my first pastor and spiritual mentor wrote me in our early years of ministry. He sent it after receiving an update from me that included a book Dennis had recently published and a few bragging points about how much our ministry had grown. I'd hoped that he, being a sort of spiritual father to us, would be proud of our success.

His reply surprised me. Rather than crowing over our outward achievements, he acknowledged them with brief kindness. Then, he wrote something like this: *As I've matured in the Lord, I've learned to esteem inward growth more than outward production. I've learned that my greatest victories are won on the inside, on battlefields no one else can see.*

Selah.

I wish now that I'd kept the letter. But when I received it, I was still so steeped in performance I didn't appreciate it. I was still too much of a *human doing* to grasp what my pastor was trying to tell me.

Thank heaven, I finally got the message. More than a decade after I threw his letter away, I grabbed onto the rope of real victory—the kind that starts on the inside, with a revelation of redemption—and refused to let go. If the fight got hard and messy, it didn't matter. If emotions and circumstances set me spinning, so what? I'd glimpsed the freedom that was mine in Christ and I refused to live without it anymore. So I set my jaw, latched onto what was mine and, like Duke going airborne, I hung in there until I won.

Today my life is as different from what it used to be as day from night. There are still more victories to be won, but I'm not slogging through the swamps anymore. I'm marching forward in joy, taking higher ground, with the enemy on the run.

And some days, I dance.

Most of the time, I just do it on the inside. But every once in a while, I do it on the outside like I did one day when Dennis and I were shopping at the mall. I don't know what got into me. Maybe I was inspired by the Righteous Brothers' tune filtering through the store's sound system. Maybe the friends walking beside us—the same couple that went with me to the Righteous Brothers' concert years ago—sparked a wave of nostalgia. Maybe I remembered how they danced in the aisle of the Will Rogers Colliseum like a couple of high school kids, and how I watched them from the shadows, yearning to be that free.

Whatever the reason, right there in the middle of the mall, I looked at Dennis, he looked at me, and we began to dance. Our friends did too. While the Righteous Brothers' crooned about losing that lovin' feelin', we proved amid gawking customers and startled store clerks that we hadn't.

Jessica, who'd been walking with us, disowned us and disappeared. She was understandably mortified.

But for once, I didn't care. Finally free enough to dance, I decided to do it.

Just because I could.

"Some Days You Dance"

DISCOVERY GUIDE

Before beginning the road to freedom, are you ready to be honest with yourself and with God? Maybe you're not quite sure if you can be brutally honest but you're willing to begin exploring the facts and weigh them against the truth. But before you answer such a tough question, take a moment to read the following scenarios and see if they describe your life:

➤ Although I faithfully attend church, read my Bible and pray, when I leave church my heart still aches because of my broken life.

➤ I know Jesus set me free but I'm still bound by fear, rejection, insecurity and shame.

➤ No one else talks about these feeling so I must be defective. Maybe it didn't work for me like it has for others. Perhaps there's something wrong with me.

➤ Am I so broken that even Jesus can't fix me?

➤ Why is it so hard?

If you identified with these feelings, don't feel bad, you're not alone. I talk to scores of people who feel too ashamed to admit that after being a Christian for years, they feel the same way. The good news is that we aren't destined to live the rest of our lives feeling that way. Nothing would bring me greater honor than taking the steps to freedom with you. Together we can look at the plain truth and get the answers needed to walk into a new life—a life free from fear, rejection, and shame. Your steps may feel shaky and uncertain, but Jesus will allow you to go at your own pace. He did that for me and He will do it for you too.

2

A Failed Journey of Inches

Now may the God of peace Himself sanctify you completely; and may your whole spirit, soul, and body be preserved blameless at the coming of our Lord Jesus Christ. He who calls you is faithful, who also will do it.

1 Thessalonians 5:23-23

Past:

1. When you were first born again, how did you expect your life to change as a result of your newfound faith? Which of these changes have taken place? Which haven't?

_____

_____

After you were born again did you believe...

☐ *From this day forward, my past is gone and it will never affect me again.*

☐ *I won't have any more problems.*

☐ *I will never have another day of unhappiness. I will always be happy.*

☐ *From now on, everything in my life will be perfect.*

☐ *Other:_____*

_____

---

2. The devil sows seeds of insecurity and inadequacy into everybody—especially Christians. Identify the areas of your life where you've struggled with those feelings. How have

you dealt with them? How have they affected your relationships (with God, family members, friends, and co-workers)?

_____

_____

Present:

1. Think about your life and write down the things you do that give you a sense of value, worth or control. Ask the Holy Spirit to reveal to you what caused this behavior and how to change these destructive patterns.

_____

_____

2. God's Word tells us that we have been set free from the lies of the devil that have kept us bound. But we often neglect to spend enough time in the Word to get it down into the bedrock of our soul. What keeps you from spending time every day in God's Word? Is it your busy schedule, a lack of desire, a lack of confidence in your ability to connect with God, or something else? Ask the Holy Spirit what steps you can take to overcome those obstacles.

_____

_____

3. Without a deep heart-revelation of spiritual truths, those truths fail to affect our feelings and behavior. For example, we may believe intellectually that God loves us while still feeling unaccepted and acting insecure. Identify a spiritual truth that you know has not yet made the journey from your head to your heart. What problems has that lack of revelation caused in your life?

_____

_____

> **If the Lord were talking with you, would He point out something like...**
>
> ☐ *You are so perfectly acceptable in My sight, why do you still feel that you must earn My love?*
>
> ☐ *You don't have to strive for perfection or prove yourself to Me. I love you for who you are.*
>
> ☐ *If you will come into My presence, I will empower you to overcome the things that have bound you.*
>
> ☐ *Other* _____
>
> _____

Future:

1. When we lack a heart revelation of how fully loved and accepted we are by God, we often try to earn that love and acceptance by our performance. What things do you do to prove yourself or gain the approval of others? How would your life change if you fully received God's love and accepted yourself for you who are?

_____

_____

2. Ask your heavenly Father to help you grasp His love for you, then spend some time in His Word and in prayer. Write down what you sense He is saying to you and any scripture verses He quickens to your heart.

_____

_____

Meditate on these scriptures about how much God loves and accepts you:

- *"We are made right with God by placing our faith in Jesus Christ. And this is true for everyone who believes, no matter who we are" (Romans 3:22).*

- *"Now there is no accusing voice nagging those who are united to Jesus Christ, that is, those whose lives are directed by the Spirit rather than by old attitudes and patterns" (Romans 8:1 BCJ).*

- *"For God took the sinless Christ and poured into him our sins. Then, in exchange, he poured God's goodness into us!" (1 Corinthians 5:21).*

- *"But God is so rich in mercy, and he loved us so much, that even though we were dead because of our sins, he gave us life when he raised Christ from the dead. (It is only by God's grace that you have been saved!)" (Ephesians 2:4-5).*

- *Other _____*

  _____

3

The Offer I Couldn't Refuse

*Come into fellowship with me if you are tired and bur-
dened, and I will refresh and release you. Take the burden
of responsibility I give you and thereby discover your life
and your destiny. I am gentle and humble; I am willing to
relate to you and to permit you to learn at your own rate;
then, in fellowship with me, you will discover the meaning
of your life. My fellowship will release you, and my companionship will direct you on your journey.*

Matthew 11:28-30
Ben Campbell Johnson Paraphrase

Past:

1. Influential people, especially our parents, sow seeds during
our childhood that shape how we perceive ourselves. Ask the
Holy Spirit to help you identify two or three such perceptions that have in some way robbed you of your freedom to
enjoy and be yourself.

Wrong thoughts and perceptions have caused me to...

☐ *...work harder and harder in a desperate attempt to earn
others' love.*

☐ *...change who I am in the hope that I can be more pleasing
to others.*

☐ *...do almost anything in order to hear the words "I love you."*

☐ *Other* _____

_____

2. How have the negative perceptions you've identified hindered your relationships with God, family members, friends, and co-workers?

_____

_____

3. To gain complete freedom in your life, you must be honest about past hurts. Ask yourself: *Have I really gotten over them? Or have I merely swept them under the rug, assuming I've forgiven those who hurt me? What old scarred-over wounds still need the healing balm of the Holy Spirit?*

_____

_____

_____

Present:

1. Jesus promises you rest and refreshing if you will simply come to Him. He allows you to set the pace and move toward a life that is so meaningful, so full of joy, so refreshing that you won't recognize it. Ask the Lord to show you some of the areas in which He wants to lead you to personal freedom.

_____

_____

> **My self-image has primarily been shaped by...**
> ☐ ...*my mother or father's opinion of me.*
> ☐ ... *the way others treat me.*
> ☐ ... *what the Bible says about God's love for me.*
> ☐ *Other* _____
> _____

2. When, in the midst of pain and darkness, you are tempted to make rash decisions and do something you will later regret, remember the story of the mountain climber. How does that story apply to you right now? In what area of your life do you most need to sit still and wait for the light and wisdom of God?

_____

_____

_____

> **I believe that God wants to lead me:**
> ☐ *...into a relationship with my family members that will be rewarding to each of us.*
> ☐ *...into a new career that more fully expresses who He created me to be.*
> ☐ *...into a closer walk with Him that my life be truly Christ centered.*
> ☐ *Other* _____
> _____

Future:

1. Jesus emphasized the importance of taking on *ONLY* the responsibilities He gives you. Any added responsibilities become like Nehemiah's rubble, cluttering your life, sapping your strength, and stopping you from doing what God specifically called you to do. Ask the Lord to show you any responsibilities you are carrying that He has not given and reveal to you how they can be removed.

_____

_____

Some of the add-ons that have cluttered my life and sapped my strength are...

☐ *... volunteering to help whenever my children's school asks me, whether I have the time or not.*

☐ *...taking on too many projects at work that require me to work 60 hours a week to finish everything.*

☐ *...being the one to answer everyone's call when they have trouble and can't seem to figure out what to do.*

☐ *Other* _____

_____

---

2. Write down a few shining moments when you have graciously turned down what would have become an add-on in your life.

_____

_____

_____

4

Love Letters in the Sand

And God saw every thing that he had made, and, behold it was very good.

Genesis 1:31

Past:

1. Ask the Holy Spirit to help you identify some of the add-ons that have robbed your life of the easy life Jesus promised.

_____

_____

_____

Examine these areas to see if you can say no to these add-ons and bring relief to your life.

☐ *Get family members to help with household chores.*

☐ *See if you can find someone else to help or volunteer at your children's school or at church.*

☐ *Allow your coworkers to do their own job and gradually reduce the amount of help you give.*

☐ *Put the needs of others in proper perspective. Become a listener rather than their problem solver.*

☐ *Other* _____

_____

---

2. The Bible says that "the living God...gives us richly all things to enjoy" (1 Timothy 6:17). If you've allowed add-ons to overburden you and leave you with no time for yourself,

you may have lost touch with the kinds of things that bring you such enjoyment. List some hobbies or fun activities you'd like to include in your schedule that would help you feel like you've gotten your life back.

---

3. Sometimes, by trying to fit the mold set by others, we get stuck in routines, work habits, and patterns that frustrate us because they don't fit our personality. Identify any area of your life where that's happened to you.

Present:

1. What changes would you make in the areas above if you broke out of the mold others have cast for you and stopped trying to perform and meet their expectations? How would things be different if you began to do things the way the Lord leads you to do them? Ask the Holy Spirit to give you the wisdom and guidance you need to begin taking steps in that direction. Write down what He tells you.

---

2. How does it make you feel to know that God took such care to provide a magnificent home for His children? God set His family plan in motion by what He said. Write down some

areas in your life in which you can begin to change what you say in order to set God's plan in motion for your life.

_____

_____

3. Spend a few minutes in prayer and ask the Holy Spirit to rewrite your personal creation story. Write down what He tells you and read it daily until it begins to replace the old story.

_____

_____

I can begin to set God's plan in motion for my life by saying...

☐ *...I am unconditionally loved and wanted by God.*

☐ *...God has a plan for my future that is filled with hope.*

☐ *...I can do all things through Christ who fills me with strength.*

☐ *... I am more than a conquer through Christ Jesus.*

☐ *Other* _____

_____

Future:

1. Take a moment to allow the Holy Spirit to show you, when in the barren winters of your life, He prepared a bridge to meet your needs. Take a moment to jot down the confidence it gives you knowing that the Lord prepared a bridge in the past. How does it give you hope for your future? Does it make you feel more significant and secure in Him?

_____

2. If the veil between heaven and earth were lifted and you could look into the Lord's eyes, what loving words would He say to you? Ask the Holy Spirit to continue to reveal them to you throughout the day.

_____

_____

_____

If I were looking into the eyes of the Lord, He would say...

☐ *I love you and accept you for who you are, not for the way others want you to be.*

☐ *I have a future planned for you that is filled with hope.*

☐ *I have built a bridge for you that will lead you to your destiny.*

☐ *Other* _____

_____

---

3. Pray the following prayer and let God's love wash away the pain, leaving in its place a divine love letter written to anyone willing to read it.

> Dearest child, I created all this for you. Apart from you, there is no reason for it. No reason for beauty, no reason for the earth at all. You, dear one, are the fulfillment of My eternal dream. You are no accident, no mistake. I planned you before the world began. I saw you while you were yet unborn and longed to have an unending love relationship with you. I have always loved you and I always will. You can do nothing to earn that love and nothing to lose it. It is yours just because you exist...just because you are My child.
>
> Forever,
> Your Father

5
The Night God Played the Jukebox

*Long ago, even before he made the world, God loved us
and chose us in Christ to be holy and without fault in
his eyes. His unchanging plan has always been to adopt
us into his own family by bringing us to himself through
Jesus Christ. And this gave him great pleasure.*

Ephesians 1:4-5

Past:

1. What outward accomplishments or works have you relied
on to help you overcome a sense of unworthiness, shame, or
a general sense of "missing the mark"?

_____

_____

**In an effort to overcome the sense of "missing the
mark," I have...**

☐ *...sacrificed my family's needs in order to help solve other
people's problems.*

☐ *...volunteered to help with church activities even when I
didn't have the time.*

☐ *...read my Bible and prayed hoping to gain God's acceptance and approval.*

☐ *...given money out of guilt instead of being led by the Lord
which caused hardship to my family.*

☐ *Other* _____

---

2. What religious misconceptions have distorted your understanding of God's love over the years? How did those misconceptions stop you from drawing near to Him?

_____

_____

_____

3. Can you remember important prayers in your past that seemed to go unanswered? How did those experiences affect your view of God and the development of your spiritual life?

_____

_____

_____

Present:

1. Remembering how passionate and personal God's love is for you, list a few things God has done recently that show you how intimately He knows you and how He is continuously pursuing a relationship with you.

_____

_____

_____

God has recently shown His love for me by...

☐ *...giving me the desire of my heart that no one knew about except me and God.*

☐ *...answering my prayer in spite of my attitude and lack of attention toward Him.*

☐ *...bringing someone into my life to share His love with me despite my lack of church attendance.*

☐ *Other* _____

_____

2. Do you have a habit of criticizing yourself for your imperfections and shortcomings? How have such thoughts hindered you from sensing how delighted God is with you?

_____

_____

_____

3. How would knowing and believing that God made you a living, breathing copy of Himself effect your future—the way you think, act, or approach challenges?

_____

_____

_____

> **If I saw myself restored to my original condition I would...**
>
> ☐ *...expect a future filled with goodness, favor, and joy.*
>
> ☐ *...no longer think of myself as a failure but a success waiting to happen.*
>
> ☐ *...believe that despite adverse circumstances, God is on my side and who dare be against me.*
>
> ☐ *Other* _____
>
> _____

Future:

1. Ask the Lord to show you areas in your life that can be improved by changing the way you have understood how God views you.

_____

_____

_____

2. God looks beyond the temporary effects of sin in your life and sees you restored to your original condition, how does this affect your fellowship and relationship with Him?

_____

_____

_____

3. When you consider this amazing message of grace, what does it inspire you to say to the Lord?

_____

_____

_____

6

The One Thing

*"But one thing is needed, and Mary has chosen that good
part, which will not be taken away from her."*

Luke 10:42

Past:

1. Describe the feelings you had when you first fell in love
with Jesus. Can you identify any ways in which your love
for Him has changed over the years? Ask the Holy Spirit
to restore the affection and child-like abandon you once had
with Him.

_____

_____

_____

2. Has your relationship with the Lord and service to Him
become driven by duty? What are some of the things that
have become duty that should be delightful and easy?

_____

_____

_____

My love for the Lord became driven by duty when...

☐ ...I thought I needed to earn God's love and approval.

☐ ...I tried to overcome guilt, shame and inadequacy.

☐ ...my drive to please people overshadowed my desire to please God.

☐ ...I felt the need to prove my worth and value.

☐ Other _____

_____

3. Remember a time when you turned a simple event of service for the Lord into something that took you away from sitting at His feet. What kinds of emotions were stirred by that event? Did it make you angry, regretful, guilty, or did you feel something else?

_____

_____

_____

Present:

1. When Martha became overwhelmed, she not only blamed Mary for her situation, she also blamed Jesus. Recall a time you became overwhelmed or stressed. Who did you blame for causing the stress?

_____

_____

_____

When I've become overwhelmed I blamed...

☐ ...*my boss for not seeing that my plate was already full without adding to it.*

☐ ...*my family for not seeing what needed to be done and helping.*

☐ ...*the Lord for allowing me to get into such stressful situations.*

☐ ...*a friend for always expecting me to solve problems that don't belong to me.*

☐ *Other* _____

_____

2. The next time you have an opportunity to enjoy the fellowship of the Lord with a group of believers, ask the Holy Spirit to show you what steps you can take to avoid falling into the Martha Syndrome. Write them down below so you can refer to them when the situation arises.

_____

_____

_____

3. We have all fallen into the trap of working for the Lord instead of spending time with Him and in His Word. Ask the Holy Spirit to show you how to keep your priorities straight. Jot down the ideas that He gives you and ask Him to help you to begin implementing them in your life.

_____

_____

_____

Future:

1. The way to avoid slipping from Mary-dom into Martha-dom is to spend time daily with the Lord and in His Word. What have been the major obstacles that have prevented you from spending quiet time in the past? How can you avoid these obstacles in the future?

_____

_____

_____

I plan to avoid falling into the obstacles that prevent me from spending time with the Lord by...

☐ *...finding a place to make my personal "prayer closet."*

☐ *...getting up a littler earlier to ensure I have personal uninterrupted time.*

☐ *...using the time the children are taking a nap to turn off the television and seek the Lord.*

☐ *Other* _____

_____

---

2. The Pharisees added 2,000 rules to what God had told His people. The devil still does that today. What are some of the struggles you face as a result of legalistic rules that others have imposed on you? Ask the Lord for the wisdom to end these obligations.

_____

_____

_____

3. Ask the Holy Spirit to show you what actions and behaviors are driving you further from the Source of life and how you can turn things around. Then pray for His empowering to do so.

_____

_____

_____

7

No Need to Hide

*For you were once darkness, but now
you are light in the Lord.*

Ephesians 5:8

Past:

1. We can all identify with the Elliot Syndrome—or what some call sin consciousness—that makes us hide portions of our past from others. What self-condemning thoughts hinder you from openly sharing your own less than perfect past?

_____

_____

_____

I have trouble putting the past behind me because I continue to ...

☐ *...focus on my past failures.*

☐ *...believe lies that were spoken over me by significant people in my life.*

☐ *...fall back into old habit patterns that I had before I was born again.*

☐ *Other* _____

_____

---

2. Describe a time in your life when you shared a secret from your past and someone responded with acceptance and compassion. Write down how it made you feel.

_____

_____

_____

3. Knowing you are a new creation is the key to leaving the Elliot Syndrome behind. What habits and patterns from your past would lose their power over you if you truly walked in the freedom that belongs to you in Christ?

_____

_____

_____

Present:

1. Sometimes we try to hide our feelings of inadequacy by becoming super-achievers in some area of life; or we attempt to cover up our inner sense of unworthiness with outward symbols of status and success. God, however, sees through those things. He knows what's really going on in our hearts. Ask Him to show you ways you've tried to hide from Him and from others and write them below.

_____

_____

> **I've tried to keep my sense of inadequacy hidden by...**
>
> ☐ *...staying so busy I don't have time to confront the issues from my past.*
>
> ☐ *...demanding outward perfection of myself in the way I dress, keep house, entertain, etc.*
>
> ☐ *...accumulating status symbols like expensive cars, designer furniture, or positions of leadership at church.*
>
> ☐ *...continually doing more and more, trying to do it better in hope of becoming the person I want to be.*
>
> ☐ *Other* _____
>
> _____

2. Adam and Eve became the first victims of identity theft when Satan twisted their thinking about what God had said to them. Ask the Holy Spirit to expose the lies Satan has planted in your mind regarding who you are in Christ and write them below.

_____

_____

_____

> **Satan—the identity thief—has stolen...**
>
> ☐ *...my sense of being righteous and acceptable in God's sight.*
>
> ☐ *...my confidence to stand before God and pray or hear His voice.*
>
> ☐ *...my child-like innocence before God and people.*
>
> ☐ *...the truth that I qualify for God's love, favor, direction and guidance.*
>
> ☐ *Other* _____
>
> _____

3. Is there anything in your past that still makes you feel guilty or ashamed when you think about it? Take time now to lift it to God in prayer and ask Him to help you receive the forgiveness and cleansing He has made available to you through the blood of Jesus. Describe what happened in you as a result of your prayer.

_____

_____

Future:

1. God loves and accepts you unconditionally even when you have sinned. How will this knowledge change the way you approach God in the future?

_____

_____

_____

I will be more conscious of...

☐ *...God's forgiveness rather than my guilt.*

☐ *...God's ability to lift me out of problems instead of my shortcomings.*

☐ *...God's commitment to deliver me out of my sin and habits.*

☐ *Other* _____

_____

2. What are some of the works you "do" in an attempt to achieve what God has already "done" for you?

_____

_____

_____

3. Recognizing that there is a personal "do" for each of us within what Jesus has already "done" ask the Holy Spirit to reveal your God-ordained individual mission-impossible. Write down the direction as He shows it to you.

_____

_____

_____

8

Good Morning, Lord

*Now the Lord is the Spirit, and where the Spirit of the
Lord is, there is liberty (emancipation from bondage,
freedom). And all of us, as with a unveiled face [because
we] continued to behold [in the Word of God] as in a
mirror the glory of the Lord, are constantly being transfigured into His very own image in ever increasing splendor
and from one degree of glory to another; [for this comes]
from the Lord [Who is] the Spirit.*

2 Corinthians 3:17-18 The Amplified Bible

Past:

1. There is a difference between being recreated in God's
image on the inside and behaving like Him on the outside.
Identify three areas in which your behavior contradicts who
you truly are in Christ.

_____

_____

_____

My behavior often conflicts with my identity in Christ...
☐ *...at work.*
☐ *...with my spouse and children.*
☐ *...when I'm around unsaved friends.*
☐ *...when someone offends me at church.*
☐ *Other* _____

_____

---

2. Ask the Holy Spirit to show you a specific situation where you would have responded differently if you'd been operating in the light of what Jesus has done for you on the cross. Ask Him how you can work with Him to renew your mind with the Word in that area so you can handle such situations better in the future.

_____

_____

_____

3. Knowing Jesus was as human as you are and that He had to grow incrementally like you do, identify a few ways in which you've grown to be more like Jesus since you gave your life to Him. Does acknowledging that growth encourage you?

_____

_____

_____

Present:

1. Since Jesus accepted and was patient with His growth process, you can be too! Are there any areas where you tend to be impatient with yourself? What are they and how would your life change if you chose to relax, allow yourself to develop at your own pace, and enjoy the process?

_____

_____

_____

2. Have you ever tried to change someone else by your own efforts, without the leading of the Lord? How did the situation turn out? What did you learn from the experience?

_____

_____

_____

3. You laugh at the distortion that an amusement park mirror makes of your reflection because your mirror at home reflects your true image. Ask the Lord to show you some things that distort your true spiritual image—the image reflected in God's Word.

_____

_____

_____

Future:

1. How does it make you feel to know that Christian success isn't defined by perfection but by perpetual growth? List some signs of growth you'd like to see in yourself in the coming weeks and months.

_____

_____

_____

2. The devil shoves his own mirror in our face in an effort to keep us trapped in sin consciousness. He likes to tell us what's wrong with us and magnify our mistakes. How has he done this to you? How can you resist him and remain confident in your true identity?

_____

_____

The devil has shoved his mirror in my face trying to make me feel...

☐ *...ashamed of my imperfect behavior.*

☐ *...inferior to others who have grown more quickly than I have.*

☐ *...inadequate and defective to do what God has called me to do.*

☐ *...guilty about being so blessed when others aren't.*

☐ *Other* _____

_____

9
Saying Goodbye to the Blame Game

*...God made you alive with Christ. He forgave all our sins.
He canceled the record that contained the charges against
us. He took it and destroyed it by nailing it to Christ's
cross. In the way, God disarmed the evil rulers and
authorities. He shamed them publicly by his victory over
them on the cross of Christ.
So don't let anyone condemn you...*

Colossians 2:13-16

Past:

1. As a new Christian, recount a time when the blame game
was a way to ease your feelings of inadequacy or guilt. How
did it feel to play a victim?

_____

_____

**Which of the following have you experienced after
playing the victim...**

☐ *...other people were in control of my life instead of being in
control of my own life.*

☐ *...it prevented me from acknowledging my need for God's
forgiveness, mercy, and grace.*

☐ *...it stopped me from receiving the love and acceptance
God was offering me.*

☐ *...it kept me imprisoned even though God had made a way
to be set free.*

☐ *Other* _____

---

2. Recount a situation in which God used His Word to teach you, reveal wrongdoing, or reset the course of your life.

_____

_____

_____

3. Recall a situation in which you blamed God for what was wrong in your life. How would you have grown in your spiritual life had you looked inward and asked the Holy Spirit to reveal where you had missed it?

_____

_____

_____

Present:

1. Relate a time when the nature of God was reflected in your behavior and instead of blaming someone, you showed them patience and made allowances for their fault because of your love for them.

_____

_____

2. Despite the circumstances in your life, what decisions can you make over your feelings and actions that will change how you respond to them—choices that will make you live a happy, fulfilled life?

_____

_____

_____

3. Recall a time when you chose to take personal responsibility to do what was right and let the chips fall where they may in spite of what it might cost you.

_____

_____

_____

After making the tough decision to do what was right...

☐ *...my personal self-respect was left undamaged.*

☐ *...my family has not lost their admiration for me.*

☐ *...my friends and co-workers know they can trust me.*

☐ *...I have maintained my personal integrity.*

☐ *Other* _____

_____

Future:

1 . How does the fact that Jesus willingly took the blame and paid the penalty for all you have done empower you to resign the role of a victim?

_____

_____

_____

> **God's willingness to take the blame for my wrongdoings helps me to...**
>
> ☐ *...freely acknowledge my sin, shortcomings, and failures.*
>
> ☐ *...have the courage to take responsibility for my actions even when they're not perfect.*
>
> ☐ *...understand that I have nothing to be afraid of.*
>
> ☐ *...realize the penalty for my sin has already been paid. I am not guilty.*
>
> ☐ *Other* _____
>
> _____

2. God is never behind feelings of guilt. Instead the Holy Spirit convicts us of wrongdoing without condemning us. Why would this knowledge encourage you to run "to" God when you sin instead of running from Him?

_____

_____

3. Explain the fundamental difference between condemnation and conviction. Who is their author; how do they affect your relationship with the Lord; how do they make you feel about yourself?

_____

_____

10

Take Charge of the Camp

There is no fear in love; but perfect love casts out fear...

1 John 4:18

Past:

1. Ask the Holy Spirit to pinpoint a time when the fear of rejection drove you to alter your behavior (either negatively or positively) in a way that would bring the acceptance you desperately craved — either from God or other people.

_____

_____

_____

The fear of rejection has caused me to...

☐ *...become a workaholic in order to prove my value to others.*

☐ *...compromise my Christian values when I'm in the company of unbelievers.*

☐ *...sacrifice my own identity and destiny to adapt to what other people want.*

☐ *...stay in the background, keeping my thoughts and ideas to myself for fear of others' disapproval.*

☐ *Other* _____

_____

---

2. Tell about an event in which you tried to determine your worth — whether you felt superior or inferior, more acceptable or less — by comparing yourself to someone else. If you didn't measure up to the other person, how did you try to do more, be more, or have more in order to feel better about yourself?

_____

_____

_____

3. God made you a one-of-a-kind individual with distinct gifts. There is no one else like you. Ask the Holy Spirit to show you what unique gifts He has given you.

_____

_____

_____

Present:

1. Imagine being able to shrug off someone's rejection because you know God completely embraces and accepts you. How does imagining that affect you?

_____

_____

_____

2. Explain why it's not your job to please people. What effect does resigning from that job have on your life? How does it free you to focus on pleasing God?

_____

_____

_____

> **Knowing I don't have to please people allows me to...**
>
> ☐ ...*become the Christian God has always created me to be.*
>
> ☐ ...*excel in the individual gifts and callings that God placed in me.*
>
> ☐ ...*stop worrying about what other people think about me.*
>
> ☐ ...*become free to please God and no one else.*
>
> ☐ *Other* _____
>
> _____

3. Explain why other people's opinion of you does not determine your value. What does determine your value?

_____

_____

_____

Future:

1. Ask the Holy Spirit to reveal to you what concrete steps you can take to build a greater understanding of your true worth and your identity in Him. How would that understanding affect your day-to-day life?

_____

_____

2. Explain why we can't live in victory over the devil by simply relaxing and letting God be responsible for everything. How has your revelation of your spiritual authority changed as a result of reading this chapter? What scriptures particularly stood out to you?

_____

_____

3. In what ways have you been living like a prisoner of war even though in Christ you've been set free? What would your life look like if you exercised your spiritual authority and took charge of the camp?

_____

_____

I need to use my God-given authority to enforce God's will in my...

☐ *...financial affairs.*

☐ *...family and other relationships.*

☐ *...physical body.*

☐ *...mind and emotions.*

☐ *Other* _____

_____

11

Never Let Go

*Therefore, do not throw away your confidence, which has
a great reward. For you have need of endurance, so that
when you have done the will of God, you may receive what
was promised.*

Hebrews 10:35-36 NASB

Past:

1. Recall a time in the beginning of your Christian life when
you grabbed hold of one of God's promises with Duke-like
determination and refused to let go.

_____

_____

_____

2. Identify a Scriptural truth you learned long ago but
neglected to implement in your life. How would things be
different now if you'd put that truth into action?

_____

_____

_____

3. Looking back, can you see what you could have done to
finish the process of revelation? What steps could you have
taken to help that truth make the journey from your head to
your heart? Are you willing to make the commitment today
to say, "That's mine and I'm going to have it in my life"?

_____

_____

_____

Present:

1. Identify and list below a few of the blessings that belong to you as promised in God's Word. Find scriptures that confirm those promised blessings and begin to meditate on them until an image is built in your heart. How will this process change your future?

_____

_____

I am committed to meditate on God's Word until I can clearly see myself with the eyes of my heart...

☐ *...in right standing with God living free from guilt, shame, and fear.*

☐ *...walking in God's blessings regardless of my imperfections.*

☐ *...living in divine health and healing.*

☐ *...sharing the Gospel with others and being a blessing everywhere I go.*

☐ *Other _____*

_____

---

2. List the three connotations included in the word "meditate." Describe how you can include each of them in your life and deepen your revelation of God's Word.

_____

_____

_____

3. In what areas have you mimicked Charlie Brown's archery by shooting the arrows of life at random and then painting bull's eyes around them, assuming they represent God's will for you? What are you going to do about seeking God's wisdom in those areas of life?

_____

_____

_____

I need a clear revelation of God's will for my life regarding...

☐ *...my job or career.*

☐ *...the church I should attend.*

☐ *...who I will marry.*

☐ *...the friends I spend time with.*

☐ *Other* _____

_____

Future:

What would your life look like if you were free from the guilt, fear, and shame that has plagued your past? How would it affect your relationships? Your job or your outlook on life?

_____

_____

2. Your imagination is one of the most important tools God has given you. Select a promise from God's Word and take 10 minutes to imagine it coming to pass in your life. What impact do you think it would have on your life if you did that every day?

_____

_____

_____

My future would be changed if I began to imagine myself as...

☐ *...more than a conqueror.*

☐ *...righteous and accepted in God's sight.*

☐ *...having a Good Shepherd who promises that I will lack nothing.*

☐ *...the recipient of God's goodness and mercy.*

☐ *Other* _____

_____

---

3. The devil is a thief who will steal your God-given inheritance. List the four methods or steps you will take in the future to bring into captivity thoughts that are contrary to God's Word.

_____

_____

_____

BOOKS BY DENNIS BURKE

Dreams Really Do Come True—
It Can Happen to You!

Develop a Winning Attitude

Breaking Financial Barriers

You Can Conquer Life's Conflicts

Grace: Power Beyond Your Ability

* How to Meditate God's Word

Knowing God Intimately

A Guide to Successfully Attaining
Your God-given Goals

The Law of the Wise

* Available in Spanish

CDs BY DENNIS BURKE

Creating an Atmosphere and
Attitude for Increase

The Transfer of Wealth—
Tearing Down Satan's Final Stronghold

The Tithe—Your Blessing
Connection

Learning to Yield to the Holy Spirit

How to Cast Off Whatever Has
Cast You Down

How to Bring Your Dreams to Life

Secrets to Developing Strength of Character

BOOKS BY VIKKI BURKE

Aim Your Child Like An Arrow

Relief and Refreshing from Stress

Transforming a Distorted Self-Image

The Power of Peace—
Protection and Direction

CDs and TAPES BY VIKKI BURKE

Pressing Through the Promise
into Possession

Burn with Passion—
Reach a Higher Level of Living

Other

practical
resources from
Vikki Burke

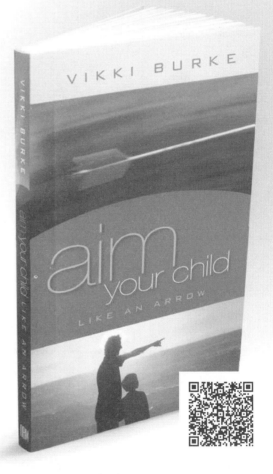

Aim Your Child Like an Arrow

"For those of you with the responsibility of raising a family, I know this book will be an invaluable tool that you will refer to many times as you seek to apply God's truths to training your children or grandchildren. Vikki is a great communicator of these truths, and her 'how to' applications are practical and insightful. In today's society with so many dysfunctional families, it is refreshing to know that the Word of God is still the answer.

Vikki Burke is a mother who has applied God's Word in raising her child. Her daughter Jessica is a young woman who reflects her parents' dedication to biblical training. She is a credit to the values they have instilled in her. As a mother and grandmother, I take the responsibility of continuing to instill the Word of God into my children and grandchildren very seriously. In reading this book, I was blessed and found fresh inspiration for ministering to my family. You will too."

—**Carolyn Savelle**

Order online today, or call toll-free **1-800-742-4050**

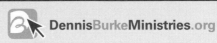 **DennisBurkeMinistries**.org

Start your day, armed with *the* Truth.

So many will begin their mornings tuning in to TV news, or fill the quiet with the empty banter of early morning secular talk shows. We all know starting off right can prepare us for victory. Why not fuel up with strength-boosting encouragement and insights from God's Word?

Following are just a few testimonies from the growing number of believers who have chosen to brighten their mornings with the light of God's Word through the DBM *Enriching Life Daily* devotional emails:

"Thank you for saying yes to the Lord and following after His heart. Your daily inspirationals are so anointed… clear, precise and Life giving. You and Dennis follow the heart beat of the Lord. Jesus continue to bless all you put your hand to and increase your circle of influence for His Kingdom. Much love in Him…"

"Thank you for this email, it was exactly what I needed today. God bless you for the work you are doing in extending God's kingdom."

"Thank you for your daily emails…they are such a blessing to me and help me with my walk with God. I look forward to them everyday and they encourage me in God's Word daily! I am so thankful for God bringing you into my life through my church. You are awesome and thank you so so much! Blessing to you both…"

testimonies

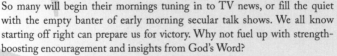

Try *Enriching Life Daily with Vikki Burke!*
DennisBurkeMinistries.org

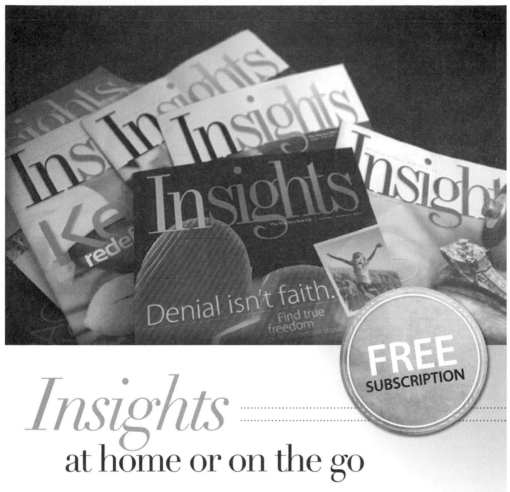

Insights
at home or on the go

Now you can choose to enjoy each issue of Dennis Burke Ministries *Insights* magazine online—or in print. If you have not yet signed up to receive your copy of *Insights* delivered to your door, follow this link for a free subscription:

dennisburkeministries.org/**insights-magazine.html**

Follow this link to begin reading immediately on your computer or mobile device:

http://dennisburkeministries.org/**insights_welcome.html**

FREE SUBSCRIPTION